FINGERPRINTS
GOD OF

WHERE HEAVEN MEETS EARTH

FINGERPRINTS
GOD OF
WHERE HEAVEN MEETS EARTH

STEPHEN J. MALLOY

EDITED BY
BARBARA L. CAMENGA

iUniverse, Inc.
Bloomington

Fingerprints of God
Where Heaven Meets Earth

iUniverse books may be ordered through booksellers or by contacting:

iUniverse
1663 Liberty Drive
Bloomington, IN 47403
www.iuniverse.com
1-800-Authors (1-800-288-4677)

ISBN: 978-1-4759-4593-5 (sc)
ISBN: 978-1-4759-4595-9 (hc)
ISBN: 978-1-4759-4594-2 (ebk)

Printed in the United States of America

iUniverse rev. date: 10/30/2012

Contents

Acknowledgments ix

Prologue xiii

Notes from the Author xxvii

Declaration xxix

Introduction xxxi

Chapter 1   Medjugorje: A Miracle for Our Times 1

Chapter 2   Called to Conversion 25

Chapter 3   Healings, Signs, and Wonders 35

Chapter 4   Pilgrimage 53

Chapter 5   The Message: What Is She Saying? 65

Chapter 6   Spiritual Warfare 75

Chapter 7   The Problem of Materialism 89

Chapter 8   The Ten Secrets, the Warnings,
             and the Chastisement 97

Chapter 9   Moral Theology, Sin,
             and Their Biblical Foundations 113

Chapter 10   God and Justice 121

Chapter 11   Medjugorje and Church Authority 133

Chapter 12 Road to Peace 151

Appendix 1 Heaven, Hell, and Purgatory 169

Appendix 2 Scientific, Psychological, and Theological Studies
            on the Six Visionaries and the Medjugorje
            Phenomenon 175

Appendix 3 Additional Statements of the Church on Matters
            Concerning Medjugorje 185

Appendix 4 How to Pray the Rosary 199

Appendix 5 Theology of Private Revelations 209

Endnotes 213

This book is dedicated to my parents, Patricia and Allen, who were my first teachers in the faith.

Acknowledgments

I would first like to acknowledge the editorial contributions of Lindael Rolstone. Lindael is a friend I met in Medjugorje in 2010. She has been on pilgrimage several times to Medjugorje from Canada. In Canada, she is a Registered Clinical Counselor (RCC), Registered Clinical Social Worker (RSW), and Registered Occupational Therapist (ROT). She is also talented with literary work. She invested a significant amount of time in reading my book and e-mailing me with many helpful comments. Lindael's recommendations helped me in several areas, in particular rewording or editing certain sections to increase the book's potential appeal to a more diverse population. In addition, she encouraged me to do more storytelling and to write more about my personal experiences. I've followed her advice. Thank you so very much, Lindael, for your kind contributions and generosity in assisting with this work.

I would also like to acknowledge my editor, Barbara L. Camenga, for helping me with this project. I also met Barbara in Medjugorje. Barbara lives in the United States and has traveled to Medjugorje from the USA seventeen times. In addition, she has had many years of writing and editing experience. So she encouraged me by offering to edit my book. Barbara's contribution was mainly in the area of content editing. She also helped me through a significant number of e-mails we exchanged as we worked toward publication. Thank you, Barbara, for your kind and generous support as we brought this project to its completion.

I would like to acknowledge my parents, Patricia and Allen, for taking the time to read my book during its formation period. Thanks, Mom and Dad, for your encouragement and affirmation concerning the contents of what you read and for making comments. I'm most grateful for the support and feedback you gave me as I moved through the stages of bringing the book to its completion.

Finally, I would like to thank everyone at iUniverse Publishing in Bloomington, Indiana, for your services and assistance in helping me to move the book through the editorial evaluation and production process. I've found iUniverse to be a very professional service in helping authors like me to obtain an objective outlook on their manuscript. They also encouraged more stories to relate my own personal experiences and that of others. They've helped me very much by making constructive recommendations and by working with me to ascertain that the book adheres to professional and industry standards.

This is the time of fulfillment. The kingdom of God is at hand. Repent and believe in the gospel.

—*Mark 1:15*

Prologue

I've written *Fingerprints of God* to explore a profound and mysterious spiritual phenomenon that began in the southeastern section of Europe during the 1980s. Millions of people have already descended upon the region, including many Americans, Europeans, and others from all over the world and from various religious denominations. I'll save most of the specific details for the introduction and the chapters to follow, but in beginning to address this matter now, let me state up front that this dynamic event is highly spiritual and undoubtedly Christian in orientation. Though it is Christian, it is not just for those who are practicing Christian faith.

It's also clear that this phenomenon speaks to atheists and nonbelievers. Certain atheists have come to either believe for the first time or believe again in God through this miracle. From what I understand as a Christian believer, God shows no partiality in His care for souls and desire to save us. Whether through this specific phenomenon of which I write or many other means, God desires that all men and women be saved and join Him eternally in heaven after death. So while stressing that this is Christian, it is without discrimination to religious backgrounds or beliefs. From this fountain of grace, all are invited to come and know more deeply the magnitude of God's love and desire to help us with our life both now and in the hereafter.

It appears that a generous outpouring of grace has been blessing this holy place in a unique way for just over three decades now.

The people who lived there were known to be devout before, but beginning in 1981, something entirely new took place that would dramatically change their once quiet and unassuming town. I'm speaking of the reported miracle at Medjugorje (pronounced "medje-ū-gore-ě"). Though many have now heard of Medjugorje, I still regularly come across people who have not heard of this town. This book is intended for any person who is open to God or who is seeking to believe in God or know him more. I'm writing with that perspective in mind. I won't assume everyone reading this knows about the story and the drama of Medjugorje. If you do, some of the facts I present will be familiar, but presented with a fresh perspective.

I base my information on numerous travels to Medjugorje and a related experience of spiritual conversion. I live in the Boston area, which has always been my point of departure for this pilgrimage. My first trip there was in 1988 and the most recent was in 2011. With these experiences and after studying four years of theology while in formation for the priesthood, I thought I'd be able to write a book on this topic. I'd also read other books and much information specifically about the Medjugorje phenomenon. I'll cite references from these sources to better document my opinions with supporting and corroborating information or facts. In doing so, I'll account for that which reliable and credible sources have said about these extraordinary happenings.

Before I get into the specifics about what's been happening in Medjugorje, some background material is important. Since this is a spiritual event, let's consider some basic theological concepts. I've indicated that Medjugorje is without question rooted in Christianity. A review of the New Testament Gospels confirms Christ's love for all men and women and that He came to earth with a desire and intention to work toward everyone's well-being and eternal salvation. Many people seek to know and understand Jesus better, but there are different and varied opinions about who Jesus is and who Jesus was. Historians won't debate that he was a historical figure who was likely crucified by the Roman government through the order of Pontius Pilate. Beyond that, many believe he was a prophet and a worker of miracles. Beyond that, the Christian belief is that Jesus is both fully God and fully human. Christians further believe he rose from the dead after the crucifixion, rejoined his disciples for a time, and then ascended to heaven forty days after the resurrection. I hold those Christian beliefs, and I'll try to explain how I was strengthened in those convictions through Medjugorje.

When I speak of God, I mean the monotheistic God of Judeo-Christian faith. I believe that Jesus is one of three persons within the one God. These three persons are God the Father, the Son, and the Holy Spirit. This is the profound and inexplicable mystery of the Holy Trinity. Jesus is believed to be the Son of God who was always with the Father in heaven before his birth on earth. Before he was conceived by the Holy Spirit in the womb of the Virgin Mary, it's believed the Son of God existed in heaven as whom the Bible calls "the Word." It is thus written, "The Word became flesh and made his dwelling among us. We have seen his glory, the glory of the one and only Son, who came from the Father, full of grace and truth" (John 1:14, New International Version).

In addition to addressing fundamental theological issues concerning the Holy Trinity and the person of Jesus Christ, it's also essential to address issues that concern the mother of Jesus, Mary of Nazareth. She is also known as the Virgin Mary and by numerous other titles. It's important to explore Mary's life and relationship with God because she reportedly has a very important role relating to the Medjugorje events. There, it's reported that Mary commonly appears in visions to a consistent group of six individuals from that area. She's reported to have been appearing and giving messages to these chosen six for thirty-one years as of June 25, 2012. Some people struggle with the issue of Mary or don't fully accept or understand her role. So the remainder of this prologue is written essentially to address these issues or questions.

Christians have been divided on issues relating to Mary for centuries. Some Protestant denominations honor her in some ways, but in a much different manner than Catholics. Roman Catholics are known to honor Mary much, and one may often associate a Catholic with praying the rosary, a Marian devotion. Eastern Rite Catholics also honor Mary very much. It is interesting that many Muslims honor the Virgin Mary. Though they see Jesus only as a prophet, they hold the Virgin Mary in high regard. Christians agree on key aspects of Mary's role in salvation history. We agree, for example, that she gave birth to Jesus in a stable in Bethlehem. Accounts of his birth, called the Nativity, are in the Bible (for example, in the second chapter of Luke). We agree that, along with her husband Joseph, Mary raised Jesus through his boyhood years.

Many of those in mainline Protestant denominations, however, believe that Catholics place too much focus on the Virgin Mary since Jesus is the one who saves us. Many Catholics, including me, often pray to Jesus through Mary. Certain Protestants don't accept that devotion because they believe we can or should go directly to Jesus. I believe it's true that we can go directly to Jesus, and they are right about that. I've gone directly to Jesus in prayer and have done this many times. This practice could not be contended from a theological or biblical point of view. At the same time, I also open myself and relate to the Virgin Mary. Like many Catholics, I pray the rosary, and I sometimes go to Mary to intercede for me with her Son. I can't explain Marian devotion fully or adequately in this prologue. I can say that Catholics do not worship Mary. This kind of "Mariolatry" is not the way our church teaches us to relate to her. They teach us to honor and reverence her as Jesus himself did. They also teach us that she's an intercessor with Christ. As such, we often unite our prayers to hers in asking her Son for what we may want or need. Yes, there are those who go over the line and *do* worship Mary. However, that's not an authentic Christian or Catholic practice. Rather, that's their issue and error since we believe worship is due to God alone.

To really obtain the best and most reliable information about the Madonna, we should look further to what's already been revealed in the Bible. In the plan of God the Father to save the human race, it was foreseen long before the Nativity that Jesus would be born of a virgin: "The virgin will be with child and will give birth to a son, and will call him Immanuel" (Isaiah 7:14). [1] In his account of the Nativity, the author of the gospel of Matthew explains that this prophecy from Isaiah is fulfilled in the birth of Jesus to the Virgin Mary. "All this took place to fulfill what the Lord had said through the prophet: 'The virgin will conceive and give birth to a son, and they will call him Immanuel,' which means, 'God is with us'" (Matthew 1:23, New International Version). It wasn't a coincidence or spontaneous decision for God to choose Mary nine months prior to the birth of Christ. The prophecy cited from Isaiah was written hundreds of years before his birth. There's no evidence that God's plan intended anyone else to give birth to the Lord Jesus Christ. It's reasonable to believe that the Lord's parents would be chosen well in advance and that his birth and upbringing would be carefully prepared. As such, it was also no accident that Joseph descended from the ancestry of King David. When the appointed time had come, God sent an angel to the Virgin to reveal that she'd been chosen to give birth to the "Son of the Most High" (Luke 1:32, NASB, or New American Standard Bible). This moment is referred to as the Annunciation. The Bible indicates that she responded first with a question. "How can this be?" She didn't understand because, as she said, "I am a virgin" (Luke 1:34, NASB). Mary consented after the angel Gabriel assured her that the conception would take place "by the Holy Spirit." [2]

In this age, I think we should ask ourselves this question: is Mary giving birth to Christ in a new way? The first birth began as a physical one with Jesus literally coming forth from the womb of Mary. The second birth culminates in all that is spiritual in our relations with Christ as he is born anew in the hearts of men. To understand the second birth, one must first comprehend the nature of Mary's relation to Jesus. She was not only his mother but was also his disciple and she was faithful to him until his death. I'll further establish in this prologue biblical support for Mary's discipleship and intercession with her Son, and also how she relates to us. I'm writing from the perspective of a Catholic but not without a respectful consideration of other viewpoints or interpretations of the Bible. When I speak of Mary giving a second birth to Christ today, it's now through her close relation to him in heaven. This is based on the premise that the glory which Mary received of being the "Theotokos" (or God-bearer) does not end with the Nativity. After she gave birth and raised Jesus, it's inconceivable that God would have said: "Thank you very much, Mary. We're all set now. We appreciate your help." Jesus lives eternally and is forever the Son of God. So likewise, Mary's motherhood and discipleship will also be honored for all ages. At the Visitation, her cousin Elizabeth declares her blessedness, providing us with a preview to these words of the Hail Mary: "Blessed are you among women and blessed is the fruit of your womb!" (Luke 1:42, NASB). In response to Elizabeth's greeting, Mary foresees that this honor is permanent: "For behold, from this time on, all generations will count me blessed. For the Mighty One has done great things for me; and holy is His name" (Luke 1:48-49, NASB). In this Magnificat prayer, she is singing God's praises, not her own, recognizing the great honor that has been bestowed upon her in having the Messiah conceived in her womb. As Mary's role took nothing from Christ's then, so too she takes nothing away from him now. He is the Redeemer, the Savior of humankind. At the same time, the Father remains pleased that, still today as before, the Virgin prepares a most efficacious way for man to encounter Christ.

In the revelations given to those reporting to see her in Medjugorje, Mary directs us to Jesus. This is just as she did at the wedding at Cana some two thousand years ago when she said in reference to her Son, "Do whatever he tells you."[3] Jesus was about thirty years old when he went to a wedding reception with Mary at Cana in Galilee. The Bible records the story in the second chapter of John's Gospel. The wine ran out, and Mary turned to her Son with concern for those running the reception. She simply said to him, "They have no more wine." [4] He said to her in reply, "Dear woman . . . my time has not yet come." [5] Jesus hadn't worked any miracles yet. Still confident he would act, Mary instructed the servants, "Do whatever he tells you." As directed by Jesus, the servants filled some jar containers with water. After drinking from one of the jars moments later, the master of the banquet said to the bridegroom, "Everyone brings out the choice wine first and then the cheaper wine after the guests have had too much to drink. *But you have saved the best for now.*" [6] Thus, we have an account of Christ's first miracle, the changing of water into wine. What is the significance of this incident as it concerns Jesus's relationship with the Virgin Mary? It seems clear that Jesus didn't disregard his mother or her plea in this instance. If Jesus considered her intentions then, one would think he also does so now. If Jesus himself did not disregard her, then I'd encourage you to reflect on this question as we move along: should we?

We're saved by Jesus alone and none other. Mary constantly prays and works toward the salvation of souls. She can thus affect a soul's salvation by leading him or her to accept, believe in, and follow Christ. For the one who says he's been saved through faith in Jesus, what need would this person have for Mary? Why would he give any heed to her, whether in Medjugorje or anywhere else? This person claims to have reached the end and goal of which St. Paul said is the basis for salvation. Some Christians believe that once they are thus saved, they're assured of an immediate entry into heaven upon death. Other Christians don't believe there's evidence in the Bible for a guaranteed entry into heaven right after death strictly because we've professed faith or salvation in Christ. It's very good to have accepted Jesus, to profess our Christian faith, and believe we've thereby been saved. However, we must consider Christ's words to these persons who sought to enter heaven but were turned away. "Not everyone who says to me 'Lord, Lord' will enter the kingdom of heaven, *but only the one who does the will of my Father who is in heaven.*" [7] In this instance, the ones who were turned away appeared to believe in Jesus, prophesied, cast away demons, and even worked miracles in the name of Jesus. Apparently, however, other aspects of their lives were rejected by Christ. Jesus replied to them, "I never knew you. Away from me, you evildoers!" [8] We can't just say we believe in Jesus. The devil himself believes in Jesus. We must also do the will of God in our lives.

There is no better example of fidelity to God's will, with the exception of Christ's own life, than that of the Virgin Mary. From the moment she consented to the conception of Jesus at the Annunciation to Christ's last agonizing moments of dying on the cross, Mary's life was a consecration of perfect obedience to the will of God. In Catholic tradition, Mary is therefore held up as a model of virtue and faith to believers. Most likely, Mary's total consecration came well before her consent to being Jesus's mother. However, the Annunciation narrative (Luke 1:26-39) is the first biblical account in which we first see Mary's faith tested and enacted. At this moment, she surrendered herself to the most sublime and challenging mission a woman could be called to accept—to give birth to the Son of God. With Joseph, they then raised and nurtured Jesus, as he matured from being a boy to manhood. Then as he died a cruel death, during which Jesus hung on a cross for hours, she stood before him on the hill called Calvary, just outside Jerusalem's city walls. Her love knew no bounds and cast out the fear of the surrounding soldiers. Just before he died, Jesus spoke a word to his mother. Referring to the "beloved disciple" standing near her, he said, "Dear woman, here is your son." [9] Speaking to the beloved disciple, he said, "Here is your mother." [10]

Several interpretations have been drawn from these significant words coming from the Gospel according to St. John. I believe that this passage also demonstrates Jesus's regard for the Virgin Mary. At the same time, he respects the presence of the beloved disciple who also stood courageously and lovingly before Jesus at the crucifixion. Catholics interpret this moment as a significant basis by which we consider the Madonna to be our spiritual mother. One reason for this is because Christians view themselves as brothers and sisters in the spiritual family of Christ. Since we view Jesus as a brother, and the beloved disciple as well, we believe that this disciple stood in for all Christians at the cross in becoming a son or daughter of Mary. As we believe she is mother to Jesus, so also we believe she's offered to be a spiritual mother to all of us. Not everyone may agree with this outlook or accept it, but I'm using the Bible in an effort to better explain my reading on our relationship with the Blessed Mary in the family of God. As with Christ, Mary loves everyone, and I believe she wants to relate to everyone as a mother and spiritual ally.

Why Thirty-One Years of Messages?

Would God be sending the Virgin Mary to the earth with messages for thirty-one years if there was not some serious reason to do so? The unprecedented series of apparitions and messages appear to be a sign of God's *mercy*, but they are also meant to prepare us for the future. I believe God has been extending many people an olive branch. This is a time of grace when all are called to repentance. This is offered so our present life will be better and so that we may attain heaven in the next. Every day, we hear tragic stories about people who fall prey to weaknesses, and they badly damage their own lives or other lives as a result. Thus, the Medjugorje message includes a constant recommendation to practice conversion. In this context, that means a conversion of heart and a repentance of whatever sin may exist in our lives. Fallen or scandalized individuals will discover through Medjugorje that they, too, can find complete forgiveness in Jesus Christ. Through Christ, anyone can renew his life, start over, and find peace. One must accept God's grace in this regard, be contrite, and accept the boundless forgiveness God gives through Jesus's dying for us. I think Mary has been sending this message for thirty-one years because not everyone responds right away. While there are many who live by faith and according to biblical standards, there are also many who do not. For those that do respond, they may drift away and come back later. For others, the Gospel message or Medjugorje's similar themes resonate at first but then can quickly fade into the background. That's because the Gospel call, like the apparition visitor, are competing with the many voices of the secular world and technology. Thus, the Virgin must keep repeating the same message like a good teacher so it will be effective despite other influences. In some way, this could be analogized with the mother who keeps knocking at her son's door to ask him to clean up his room. She keeps waiting for a reply, but he can't hear her because he's listening to his iPod.

What happens when civilization drifts away from God? What happens when man does things his own way without considering the ways of God? Eventually, it leads to some kind of a disaster. All we have to do is pick up a newspaper or go on to CNN. I think there are negative consequences not just for one's individual life, but for the wider society. Collectively, our drifting away from God's ways can even affect our natural environment. Is it just me or has something been out of order with the natural environment? We've heard more often during the last twenty years of tragic natural disasters in many places. According to MSNBC, 2011 was the costliest year on record for property damage from natural disasters. According to the news report, "the first six months saw $265 billion in economic losses . . . well above the previous record of $220 billion set for all of 2005 (the year Hurricane Katrina struck) . . . according to Munich Re, a multinational that insures insurance companies."[11] Is it just about the so-called global warming? Should we have listened more to Al Gore? Is it about La Nina, El Nino, or other meteorological trends? People also blame this on greenhouse gases or come up with other natural explanations. These events are also signs of the times. The large number of wars during the last hundred years, along with their related violence, have also been signs of the times. What do all these troubles and calamities mean? People with eyes of faith can see and understand a meaning beyond the natural. There exists a stepped-up battle between the forces of good and those of evil. God wills and creates the good. Despite not causing the evil, God allows evil to coincide for mysterious reasons. I'm not saying the increase of such things mean the end of the world. Our Lady of

Medjugorje has not come to talk about the end of the world. In the twenty-fourth chapter of Matthew's Gospel, we find these words of Jesus as he warns his disciples not to be misled about when the end comes:

> For many will come in my name, saying, "I am the Christ," and will mislead many. You will be hearing of wars and rumors of wars. See that you are not frightened, for *those things* must take place, but *that* is not yet the end. For nation will rise against nation, and kingdom against kingdom, and in various places there will be famines and earthquakes. But all these things are *merely* the beginning of birth pangs. (Matthew 24:5-8, New American Standard Bible)

Medjugorje is a call to conversion and peace. It's not about disasters in our personal life, wars, or disorders in the natural environment. Quite the opposite, Medjugorje spells out the pathway to our peace and order for the wider world. There cannot be peace in the world, the Virgin said, until individuals first find peace within themselves and with those close to them. We can't have much peace with God if we're harboring anger toward someone else. At some point, we have to forgive them. There's no other way. Will there really be peace in the world if the person praying for this intention can't find peace within himself, in his own home, or with his neighbor or coworkers? Peace isn't just about me and God because we're all connected. If love is cut off by bitterness or hostilities, we must find some way to get beyond that. Let's not be held hostage emotionally or spiritually by some abusive person or organization. Neither they nor their actions are worth the real estate we may be granting them in our souls.

Medjugorje and Conflict

Not everyone agrees about my view that Medjugorje is a peace plan from heaven being mediated by the Virgin Mary, working through six visionaries. I experienced such disagreement while studying philosophy and theology for five years at a Catholic seminary. The conflicts with certain seminarians and priests were difficult to understand because Medjugorje seemed solid to me in a Catholic and Christian context. One priest-professor said in class that, in one sense, it "doesn't matter" if she's appearing or not. I remember being offended by that. Other priests or seminarians made strong suggestions to me that the reported visions are not really that important from a theological viewpoint. I didn't like hearing that either. Overall, it was very much downplayed and rarely discussed. Not everyone was so dismissing at the seminary, and I did find some other seminarians who were more positive about Medjugorje. I don't know how the seminary addresses Medjugorje or other private revelations now, as it's been some time since I completed studies there. As Christian believers, we should develop greater unity about the purpose and significance of these events. That has come about slowly, and the matter can still be somewhat controversial, with differing points of view. While some welcome and embrace the reported Marian intervention, others don't pay any attention to it. I know the various positions, positive and negative. Antagonists commonly react by saying: "I have Jesus. I read my Bible. I'm going to church. Don't bother me with that." Others may complain, "She always says the same thing! How long has that gone on for? What does she want from us? . . . We have the church, we have the sacraments. Why should I listen to her?"

The visionary Ivan Dragićević gave the following response to these kinds of reactions: "Yes, we have our church. We do have the Holy Bible. We have our sacraments. Our Lady asks one question in reply, 'My dear children, do you, actually, do you live everything that you have?'" [12]

Time will tell to what degree the Medjugorje event matters. In the meantime, the apparition visitor seems to have been really helping the cause of the church by drawing many souls to Christ and to church pews. Nothing's been found in the content of the reported Marian message that's contrary to Catholic or Christian faith or morals. The Madonna asked us to increase prayer and renew fasting, something certain churches have gotten away from. I wouldn't get overwhelmed by the invitation to fast, but rather come to understand the message in its entire context by reading of it further in chapters 5 and 6. The other themes of her message, which include faith, conversion, and peace, are better explained in chapter 5. If somebody gets tired of hearing reports about these visions or messages, it's better that they accept them for the sake of those souls who could otherwise be lost without them. Not everybody's reading their Bible and not everyone knows Jesus. How many people are unchurched? Many lost souls have discovered God through this channel of grace and repented of a formerly sinful lifestyle. Others, who weren't necessarily lost, still benefitted by deepening and strengthening their life of prayer or faith. Medjugorje's not just a welcoming center for the lost and those not practicing faith. It's also for active believers to help with their life situation and to provide graces for their spiritual journey.

Now let us move forward to the exploration of this great modern-day miracle, which I believe transcends the scope of human explanations. I pray you'll also discover the *fingerprints of God* on the pages you read. Does *heaven meet earth* in Medjugorje, as my subtitle indicates? While I believe heaven meets earth in many ways and in a great many places every day, I believe the meeting place at Medjugorje has some extraordinary significance to it. I ask and invite you to continue reading that I may further explain how.

Notes from the Author

I'm happy that you have chosen to pick up and begin reading my book. I would like to recommend reading the introduction before moving along to chapter 1 and the following chapters. The introduction is intended to help the reader understand the chosen title, *Fingerprints of God: Where Heaven Meets Earth*. It is also especially useful for readers not familiar with the spiritual phenomenon that is described throughout the book and identified in the next paragraph. Familiar or not, the introduction is good foundational material for anyone and will help prepare you for what comes afterward. The prologue is also recommended reading for anyone but is offered in a special way to provide some essential basics with respect to theology and other issues that pertain to God. These basics include an introductory discussion about the person of Jesus Christ and how he is also viewed as being divine in addition to being human. Further, the prologue explores the person of the mother of Jesus, the Virgin Mary. In doing so, it considers Mary's life of faith and discipleship on earth, her role in heaven, and how she relates to us.

This book chronicles certain details, events, and personal experiences regarding ongoing reports of supernatural activity taking place in Medjugorje, Bosnia and Herzegovina, since 1981. In expressing opinions on the matter at hand concerning such events, this author does not intend to preempt the final judgment of those authorities in the Catholic Church who are still investigating these happenings and have responsibility for judging the supernatural character of the reported private revelations. In the meantime, therefore, what is expressed in this book represents my opinions based on a lived faith experience and based on the testimony of others who have also been affected in the realm of faith and spiritual growth through Medjugorje.

Declaration

The *Nihil Obstat* and *Imprimatur* are no longer required for publications that deal with private revelations, provided that they contain nothing contrary to faith and morals.

Introduction

Have you watched, as I have, episodes of the TV shows *Law & Order* and *CSI: Miami?* For those not familiar, these are popular American crime dramas. Did you notice how important fingerprints are when collecting evidence in the battles of law enforcement against crime? When a person's fingerprints or DNA match those found at the crime scene, detectives strengthen their case against a particular suspect. Throughout this book, I'll be working to strengthen a much different kind of case. This case isn't about crime or wrongdoing. In choosing the title *Fingerprints of God,* I intend to say, by way of analogy, that I believe God has been leaving his own marks on this modern world in a unique and extraordinary way. His "fingerprints," if you will, are detectable. My intent is to persuade you why I believe this is true.

This isn't *CSI Miami, Law & Order,* or *Perry Mason* and I'm not a detective, police officer, or attorney. I'm a priest and this is a true story. I believe this story concerns an ongoing supernatural drama. I'll make a case that God has been doing something truly benevolent for humankind through a lengthy intervention that has spanned just over three decades now. I'll present facts and evidence to support these views. Fortunately, what we have is not a crime. If it were, we could only accuse God of love. I find reasonable cause to argue that the mercy of God has been poured out in a rather exceptional and unusual way in modern times. I'm writing of a spiritual phenomenon that, by its conclusion, will surpass the intrigue and fascination of any TV show, movie, or detective story ever created. My projection is that whoever judges this case will find God guilty. He'll be found guilty not only of love but also of offering us a much better life, salvation, and, ultimately, eternity in heaven. If I *was* an attorney and God *were* on trial for love, I'd have to join the prosecution rather than the defense. I'm convinced that God is a repeat offender, having committed these caring acts many times over.

What's really on trial though is not God but a certain spiritual dynamic from a remote area that has intrigued a great many people. Also on trial are six people from that same area who persistently claim that heaven has been speaking to them. I'll try to persuade you, the reader, that what's taken place is a miracle and those who have been thus affected have been touched by a divine hand. I've discovered his fingerprints, marks of heaven that have left their impressions on countless souls.

Let's switch the charges and defendant from the previous analogy. Instead of God being on trial for love, let's just say that these happenings, this spiritual phenomenon to which I've referred is on trial instead. Because it is. It's charged with making assertions that heaven is speaking to earth—in these days, to human beings presently living. If this was a court case and the prosecution was trying to prove that heaven was not speaking to earth, I'd have to take the role of defense attorney because I believe the opposite is true. I'll lay out my cards, show you the fingerprints I've uncovered, and encourage you to come to your own conclusions about what's presented. Like a jury, you might choose to weigh the testimony, consider the evidence, deliberate, and decide whether you also believe it's for real.

A judge may likely respond, "Okay, counselor, where are you going with this? What exactly are you talking about, this 'spiritual drama.'"

Well, Your Honor, let's first take a look at where the alleged heavenly fingerprints were found. A detective must first go to the place where the incident he's looking into was reported to occur. Older folks may remember Peter Falk from *Columbo* or Sergeant Joe Friday from *Dragnet*. Would either crack the case by staying inside his office? They went to where the alleged action happened, and they questioned people who were suspected of having something to do with it. I did travel to the place where heaven was meeting earth in a special way. I listened to the talks and testimony of these people who originally gave witness to these happenings in Europe and still do today.

I went over during the summer of 1988 to the country of the former Yugoslavia. I just wanted to see for myself what was happening and whether or not it seemed legitimate. I had heard that something very spiritual was taking place and I was open and curious. So off I went, flying from Boston into Croatia and then taking a bus ride from there into the former Yugoslavian province, Bosnia-Herzegovina. At the time, Croatia and Bosnia were still sections of Yugoslavia. I was with family, so I didn't feel quite so alone in this land, unknown to me and still under Communist rule. We spent a week there at the end of June. By the end of the seven-day stay, I was convinced that God was at work here in a manner I hadn't expected or experienced before. I learned that what was happening wasn't just for people living "over there." If what's been said can be proven true, this also appears to be for the whole world.

I'm writing about the thirty-one-year-old phenomenon that's come to be known as Medjugorje (pronounced "medje-ū-gore-ĕ"). This is a town located in the southwestern section of the now sovereign nation Bosnia and Herzegovina. A little geography may help. The map on page xxx shows where Bosnia-Herzegovina is located within the Balkan Peninsula. You can fly into Bosnia's capital, Sarajevo, from various European cities. A flight from Munich to Sarajevo is about an hour and a half. Medjugorje is then a two-and-a-half-hour bus ride from there. The Adriatic Sea separates Italy to the west and Croatia and Bosnia to the east.

Medjugorje was a simple agrarian community of some four hundred families when the mysterious phenomenon began there during the summer of 1981. Many of the people lived off of tobacco and grapes harvested in the fields. Due to constant visits from pilgrims and the widespread

Central Balkan Region

building of pansions and hotels, the simplicity of this area is not the same now. At the same time, the place remains a peaceful enclave for retreat in the midst of our busy world. Medjugorje has been successful in drawing a great many people from all over the globe to come and visit this special town. I'm only one of millions of people who have gone on pilgrimage there in recent years. Statistics account that more than 28 million people have attended church services there since 1985.[13] Its popularity would not have grown if the many people affected did not experience grace and peace through Jesus Christ. This is what I witnessed from being there. I've spoken with many others who've witnessed the same dynamic. The vast majorities go with spiritual motives, and we should consider why so many have converged on this place. Though some are just curious tourists, most who go there are seeking peace or special graces of some sort. Many pilgrims desire stronger faith, healing, or a much-needed answer to prayer.

These are the kind of graces that only God can give. Medjugorje's popularity comes mainly from people who have more easily discovered these graces through this experience. This happens either directly by being there or by reading a book, hearing a talk, or watching a video on it. All three persons of the Godhead (the Father, Son, and the Holy Spirit) have a significant role in our spiritual life. Grace originates from the Father God, the first person in the Trinity. Grace comes through the second person, Jesus, his only Son. It's then transmitted to us by the Holy Spirit, the third person. Let's consider how Medjugorje, in particular, has been anointed from above by this Holy Trinity—the Father, Son, and the Holy Spirit.

At Medjugorje, God has showered his graces on many through the lengthy presence and constant intercession of the Virgin Mary. To gain a better understanding of why Mary is a conduit and mediatrix of God-given graces, it's important to read the prologue which establishes a foundation for this. At Medjugorje, she said that she prays and asks God for all graces obtained for us. As this can be a matter of differing opinions among Christians, I try to address those sensitive issues in that section. This is provided to help better understand the role of Mary in a historical and biblical context. It should not surprise us so much though that God has chosen to work through the Holy Mother. Is this not the way by which the Father first chose to send his Son, Jesus, into the world? Why, then, would it be a struggle to accept if the Lord still chooses the Holy Virgin as a gracious means by which he works out his plans relating to Christ? Six people of the Medjugorje region, all adults now, report in tandem that they've been seeing and speaking with the Virgin Mary for thirty-one years in this very spiritual town. According to them, the Holy Mother has been calling the world to repentance and conversion by transmitting many messages through them. There are four women and two men who claim to see her in Medjugorje regularly. They're often referred to as the "visionaries" or the "seers." The women are Mirjana, Ivanka, Marija, and Vicka; and the two male visionaries are Ivan and Jakov. They're all in their forties. They were between just ten and sixteen years old when they first reported seeing the Mother of Jesus. I've seen the visionaries in person and heard them speaking publicly many times. They are authentic and consistent. They come across as sincere, and they've been persistent in making this public witness all these years. They maintain their position despite many public pressures, frequent questioning, and every kind of testing and evaluation by the Catholic Church. In the earlier years, they also faced harassment from local police, and the Communists tried to restrict and clamp down on their activities.

During my first pilgrimage, I learned of certain messages the Virgin Mary has given all of us. Upon returning home, I practiced these spiritual counsels, which the visionaries reported to come from heaven. When I've done so, I strengthened my faith and grew closer to God. So I came to see both the message and reported messengers as reliable and good. Growing up, I'd been taught many things about God and went to church each Sunday. Something was missing though, and Mary took me deeper. By the time I was twenty-five, I decided to make a second pilgrimage to Medjugorje. I saw several things on that pilgrimage that I could not explain.

I believe these were meant to strengthen my faith and I write about them in chapter 3. After describing numerous healings of illness that people have reported through Medjugorje, I describe in that chapter the signs that I saw, as well as signs and wonders others have seen. Looking back, I can see that my first two trips to Medjugorje seemed to have impacted me the most. So I include stories, especially in chapters 2 and 3, of what I experienced during those earlier days. I would return to Medjugorje nine additional times after the second trip, with the most recent visit being in May of 2011.

Along with the introduction, chapters 1-4 are meant to orient the reader to understand the Medjugorje phenomenon. I do this both from describing personal experiences and also by providing facts and objective information. Chapter 4, for example, is primarily factual information about the experience of going on pilgrimage to Medjugorje. However, I also describe this by explaining what I've actually seen and done there. Chapters 5, 6, and 7 are essentially a presentation of the most significant elements of the Medjugorje message that has reportedly been communicated by the Madonna. Chapters 5 and 6 focus on five central spiritual themes and practices that are recommended, while chapter 7 warns of the dangers of materialism. Chapter 8 is devoted to explaining the so-called ten secrets, which have been revealed to the visionaries about the future of the world. Chapters 9 and 10 apply and compare Medjugorje's message in a practical way to the Bible, the teachings of Christ, and the Ten Commandments. Chapter 11 is a thorough study of the statements and outlook of those authorities in the Catholic Church investigating the described phenomena. The church has devoted a great deal of time and effort during the last thirty-one years in testing and following these events, so I wanted to provide a chapter on that subject alone. The book concludes with chapter 12, a summary chapter that attempts to bring everything together and considers the whole of this event.

I use certain titles that relate Mary to Medjugorje, thereby reflecting my personal belief that the Virgin Mary has been active in this unique fashion there in recent decades. These titles do not intend to suggest that the church has declared officially its belief in the Madonna's appearances. Neither have they concluded that it is not her. The titles I've used include Our Lady of Medjugorje, the Virgin Mary, the Madonna, the Mother of Jesus, the Queen of Peace, the Holy Mother, and several others. The local faithful in Medjugorje commonly refer to her in Croatian as the Gospa. Not all people of faith agree when it comes to accepting or believing everything the visionaries have said about this reported heavenly visitor. The point of contention is usually whether the Madonna has actually appeared this long and communicated as many messages as she's reported to have sent, literally in the thousands. Others will ask the question "What need would I have of this Marian intervention anyways?" Even if it is true, some may say, "I already have Jesus." The book will further explain how Christ is the central focus of Medjugorje. Mary takes nothing away from Jesus and she doesn't want to be the center of attention. She diverts that to her Son.

Though Medjugorje has a very Catholic orientation, "Our Lady of Medjugorje" is ecumenical. People of various faith persuasions are welcomed and have been affected positively by this spiritual place, including those of Protestant, Jewish, and Muslim backgrounds. Mary excludes nobody, and so her messages are meant to invite all to discover greater peace through our prayerful union with God and through more harmonious relations with one another. Her ecumenism is reflected in these words the Virgin Mary reportedly gave to the visionaries in 1984: "Certainly, all religions are not equal, but all men are equal before God, as St. Paul says . . . . Those who are not Catholics are no less creatures made in the image of God, and destined to rejoin someday, the House of the Father. Salvation is available to everyone, without exception. Only those who refuse God deliberately are condemned. To him who has been given little, little will be asked for. To whomever has been given much, very much will be required. It is God alone, in his infinite justice, who determines the degree of responsibility and pronounces judgment" (A Friend of Medjugorje, *Words From Heaven*, 7th edition, Sterrett, AL: St. James Publishing by Caritas of Birmingham, 1996, 162-3). In commenting on this significant statement, one should not be presumptuous in thinking salvation is guaranteed. That is not what this means. Salvation is *available* to everyone because God wills all men and women to be saved. That salvation is available, however, does not mean it will happen for everyone or that all are accepting it.

Each chapter closes with other messages of the Madonna and some chapters include additional words she's communicated. The most important themes are faith, conversion, prayer, forgiveness, and reconciliation. We're asked to believe firmly in God, to repent of past sins, to forgive and love one another, to pray often, go to church, and read the Bible. In addition, fasting has been recommended. However, as with the other messages, it's important to understand them in their entire context. To assist this, chapters 5 and 6 are devoted to explaining these messages in greater detail. Together, these practices are designed to grant us peace.

According to the six seers, their visions will continue until all six have received each of the so-called ten secrets. These are certain events to occur in their own lives, in the village of Medjugorje, and in the wider world. Three of the six have received all ten, and the other three have nine and are waiting for the tenth. Though most information is held in strict confidence, the visionaries have been permitted to divulge certain information about the general nature of these events. The secrets are to be revealed one by one, just *before* they are to take place. The visionary Mirjana Dragićević-Soldo and a priest of her choosing have a special responsibility as it concerns the transmission of the secrets to the rest of us. The greatest specificity we have about an individual secret is that it will be a physical, permanent, and indestructible sign to be left in Medjugorje on Podbrdo, a rocky hill that is part of a larger hill called Crnica. The Virgin revealed that this physical sign is essentially for atheists and that we should not await its appearance before choosing for repentance, conversion, or amendment of our lives. Mary said, "When the sign comes, it will be too late for many" (ref. note 58). Some warnings will precede the sign, and a synopsis of these events is better described in the eighth chapter. The seventh secret, a chastisement, was eliminated thanks to prayer and fasting. The tenth secret, also a chastisement, will happen according to Mirjana. This is because, as Mirjana explained, "We cannot expect the conversion of the whole world" (ref. note 110).

How should we respond in faith to God, the Bible, Jesus, Medjugorje, and the Blessed Virgin? What do we make of all this? What do we make of Jesus in the first place? Will we follow Jesus, and surrender ourselves to him and his mercy, in order to achieve peace on earth and eternal salvation? These choices are ours to make and we're free to make them. We have set before us life and death, good and evil, heaven and hell. The decisions we make each day affect which direction we turn toward. If we've made mistakes, there's still time to change. Jesus forces nobody and so it is with Mary. They're with us to aid us in the struggles and battles of the earthly and spiritual life. In recent years, many have heard reports—maybe from a magazine, a friend, or the media—that the Holy Mother was appearing to someone or to a group of people. How many listen? How many care? Again it's based on our faith how we respond and whether we even believe this has been happening. God gives us free will, and within that freedom, we choose whether to accept Christ or reject him. We also choose whether to accept his mother or reject her.

Heavenly wonders seem to go uninterrupted at Medjugorje, even when faced with formidable foes. Powerful people have tried to stop it. When the visions began in 1981, the Communist government of the former Yugoslavia was still in power in this region, and they tried to clamp down on the public furor and gatherings of the faithful. Eventually, the Communist state disintegrated in that locality, and Yugoslavia broke up into a number of independent nations. Medjugorje became part of the Federation of Bosnia and

Herzegovina. Large crowds still gather there in places where the Communists had forbidden the people to congregate.

Ironically, Medjugorje's foes have also included certain Catholic diocesan clergy of the region in which Medjugorje is located. Chapter 11 documents the broad perspectives, both spiritual and political, that have characterized the voices of the local church authority on this matter. Among these voices in Medjugorje's diocese (of Mostar-Duvno), there's been a highly political conflict and relationship issue, historically, between the diocesan clergy of the Medjugorje region and the Franciscan order that runs the Medjugorje parish, St. James Church. One has to wonder how and whether this may have affected the statements and approach of the local bishop concerning Medjugorje. The two bishops that have been in authority since '81 have been consistently negative in their view as to whether we're dealing with heavenly visions or messages. However, it's important to read all of Chapter 11 in order to obtain a fuller picture concerning the two bishops' views.

Eventually, the Vatican chose to expand the scope of Medjugorje's investigations beyond the opinion of the local bishop and his team of advisors. According to numerous sources, the cardinal who reportedly took away the local bishop's authority on the Medjugorje deliberations was Cardinal Josef Ratzinger, now Pope Benedict XVI. As chapter 11 documents, Ratzinger took that action in 1987, passing authority on Medjugorje to the wider body of Yugoslavian bishops (and later the bishops of Bosnia-Herzegovina). The investigation was in the hands of these local bishops for some twenty years. They found nothing in the content of Mary's reported words contrary to faith or morals. They officially declared Medjugorje to be a holy place, a sanctuary, and a place of prayer where the faithful are free to go on pilgrimage. They neither confirmed nor denied the supernatural character of the apparitions. A special Vatican commission took over the work of investigation in 2010. It's headed by Cardinal Camilio Ruini. Cardinal Ruini is an Italian cardinal of the Catholic Church. At the time of this book's completion, the commission was calling the six visionaries over for interviews in Rome. The commission is expected to report their conclusions to the CDF before the end of 2012. The CDF is an arm of the Vatican that governs matters of faith and doctrine. It stands for the Congregation for the Doctrine of the Faith.

Though the church has not been inclined to hurry a final determination about the apparitions per se, they look upon the spiritual fruits of these events positively. They're pleased with the many conversions and the strong atmosphere of prayer. They likewise acknowledge positively the great number of those who have repented of past sins. When referring to private revelations such as these, they also remind the faithful that we already possess in the Word of God, the Bible, all necessary saving truth. This saving truth concluded with the life, teachings, death, and resurrection of Jesus as recorded in the Gospels of Matthew, Mark, Luke, and John. Such saving truth is also expounded upon and further clarified in the writings of St. Paul and others who gave testimony to Jesus's life, Gospel, and works in the New Testament.

Theology classifies the experience of the Medjugorje visionaries as "private revelations." Theologians disagree concerning their significance. The renowned Jesuit theologian Karl Rahner (1904-1984) taught that private revelations have their significance, and if we consider his words, their importance may be more than some thought: "The act of faith is connatural with the fact that God has spoken—publicly through Jesus Christ or privately through the prophet He has chosen."[14] The imperative "meaning of private revelations," he said, is "to help Christianity act in a particular historic situation." [15] He goes on to write: "Contrary to the fact that the revelation is ended, the prophetic element in the Church has its significance which cannot be substituted or replaced by the theological theory, human wisdom, and understanding of the Church's teaching authority and mysticism." [16] It's of significant value, then, if Mary accentuates parts of Christ's revelation that need emphasis and repetition for our times. "We ignore this voice to our detriment," says Franciscan priest Father Svetozar Kraljevic, OFM. Father's article on this matter appears in appendix 5, and I also would like to credit him for my quotes from Karl Rahner. The Bible, too, instructs us not to despise prophecies but to test them and retain what is good. "Do not quench the Spirit; do not despise prophetic utterances; but examine everything carefully; hold fast to that which is good" (1 Thessalonians 5:19-21) [17] Most believers accept the good fruits of Medjugorje, but there are still those who don't likewise believe that the reported visions are from heaven. For this outlook, we must also consider these words from the Bible: "For there is no good tree which produces bad fruit nor, on the other hand, a bad tree which produces good fruit" (Luke 6:43).

What is Medjugorje about? The Gospa, Mary, speaks to the visionaries of a great plan that has been in the works and still is. Could it be that Christ has sent the Madonna to reveal a peace plan from heaven? In view of the Blessed Virgin's close relationship with her Son and her unwavering fidelity in cooperating with the plan of God in her life, Mary is a most fitting person to be chosen in these latter days to be this prophetic figure. Through her work and love, she prepares for Christ to be born anew in the hearts of men and women. The intervention at Medjugorje appears to be a sustained and consistent effort, communicated and mediated by the Virgin Mary, to bring humanity to salvation and peace through Jesus Christ. Reflected in the many words she's said to the visionaries, she constantly prays and intercedes before her Son and is trying to bring as many people to him as possible. Essentially and most importantly, we're asked to believe in Jesus, whom the Father sent to save us. We're also asked to live as he taught. If we miss the connection of Mary's visitation to our saving relationship with Christ or if we don't understand or accept the key themes she's conveying, we'll miss the central reasons why she has come and been with us this long.

Okay, allow me to complete this introduction by circling back to our original courtroom drama and analogy. Your Honor and members of the jury, this concludes the opening arguments on behalf of the reported miracle at Medjugorje. I've thereby begun to lay the case before you on the side of the defense. There is an adversary, an opposing side. Medjugorje has those arguing against its authenticity. There are also the naysayers, those who say it's not that important even if the visionaries are telling the truth. There's even those who've suggested this it's all been made up or that it's a trick of the devil. I wish to present evidence to the contrary and respectfully ask for a fair hearing. I want to establish that this plan of heaven has mattered all along and that the only ones who could have orchestrated it are heavenly beings. Further, I will present the results of scientific testing which concluded that the visionaries are not lying. Appendix 2 provides the results of scientific and medical tests which concluded that the visionaries are genuinely seeing someone external and visible only to them. For those who say it doesn't matter—even if the visionaries are being honest—nothing could be further from the truth. Has not the church and the world needed this divine intervention very much? In a time that has had much darkness, I believe heaven has been shining more light. Where there has been sin, grace has abounded all the more. It's my case, Your Honor, that in order to help us, heaven has been speaking to earth and has been touching souls in an unprecedented fashion. In chapter 1, I will call in my first six witnesses, the visionaries. For those who do not yet believe me, please read further. I'm confident that you, too, will uncover the fingerprints of God.

"A great sign appeared in the sky, a woman clothed with the sun, with the moon under her feet, and on her head a crown of twelve stars"[18] (Revelation 12:1).

Chapter 1

Medjugorje: A Miracle for Our Times

In late June 1981, the Cold War was still in effect, and Ronald Reagan had just begun his first of eight years in office as president of the United States. Several months before, just sixty-nine days into his first term, Reagan was shot by a mentally ill man in an assassination attempt on March 30, 1981. An assassination attempt on Pope John Paul II wouldn't come much later. The Holy Father was in his third year of serving as the Roman Pontiff when he was shot four times by a Turkish gunman in St. Peter's Square on May 13, 1981. Fortunately, both survived. In their respective roles, both Reagan and John Paul II exercised significant leadership in helping to bring down the Iron Curtain, not to mention many other important accomplishments. The Cold War, which began around 1945, was finally thawing. We saw this most vividly illustrated by the tearing down of the Berlin Wall. This structure separated east and west Germany. Divided by socialist rule on the east side versus a democracy in the west, Germany was experiencing reunification, and the dividing wall became no longer necessary. In late 1989, their government permitted east Germans to cross over the wall to the other side. As they did, they celebrated unity with west Germans, and many chipped away at the structure in a symbolic show of victory over the previous division.

Why am I turning the clock back to the 1980's? I'm about to get to that, but first, can you recall what were you doing in the summer of 1981? Were you working then or were you in school? Had you begun your retirement? Had you been born yet or perhaps this was the year or decade you were born? Do you remember what you did that summer? Did you have the summer off, travel, or go away somewhere? Were you single or married? As for me, I was a boy who had just begun his summer vacation from school. I call to mind this year because I believe a great miracle began to take place in June of that year. I wouldn't hear of the miracle until seven years later.

I decided on the title *Fingerprints of God* because, absent divine intervention, I don't see how the many good things described in this book could have happened. I'm speaking metaphorically since I obviously don't have God's physical fingerprints. However, I believe I've come across many marks of a supernatural origin. In the paragraphs to follow, I present the story of how and where it all began. In law enforcement, detectives search for fingerprints at the scene of the crime. My search was for something far different. I was searching for God. I discovered him in a village lying between mountains and hills. As I describe the "fingerprints" I've uncovered, I'll try to persuade you that we can narrow down the cause of these good effects to acts of heaven. Such evidence is spread out over the chapters I've written. I'll make arguments that heaven started this miracle and that it's not yet over. This is a place *where heaven meets earth* in a unique and profound way every day. I'd like to call in my first six "witnesses." They were children who were growing up in that locality. They felt the touch of God and each one saw a beautiful lady who said she came from heaven. Their lives would never be the same again.

The next pages account for what exactly happened to the six young people during the first three days of the visions in 1981. It tells the story of how this began and how this group of six was formed and chosen by the Virgin Mary. Following this, the remainder of the chapter explores the Medjugorje event in a broader context. This first includes the positive assessment of numerous theologians. I'll then address the challenge and competition the Blessed Virgin has faced in addressing the modern secular culture. The chapter concludes with how the local bishop reacted to Medjugorje initially, and why he later changed his views.

The First Day, June 24, 1981

(Refer to endnote nineteen to reference sources for information and quotations used concerning the first day of the visions, June 24, 1981.)

Halfway around the world from where I live in America, two teenage girls were walking together. They were out of school that day and were just talking near a hill called Crnica in the former Yugoslavia. This was in the small town of Medjugorje. In Croatian, Medjugorje means "between the hills." The two girls walked toward the hill on a hot summer's day. Walking along, talking, playing—these are activities that teenage girls would ordinarily be doing on a day off. However, they were about to experience something that was anything but ordinary. Fifteen-year-old Ivanka Ivanković was the first to see something unusual. Looking two hundred meters up the hill in the section called Podbrdo, she saw a white silhouette, a luminous figure. She said to her friend, sixteen-year-old Mirjana Dragićević, "Mirjana, look, the Madonna!"

"Come on! Do you think Our Lady would appear to us?" Mirjana said, waving her hand skeptically.

Despite Ivanka's belief, Mirjana persuaded her to move on from the hill and they continued walking. They met up with a twelve-year-old-girl named Milka Pavlović. Milka asked Ivanka and Mirjana to help her tend sheep. They agreed and, while walking together, returned to the Crnica hill in the section known as

Podbrdo. As they came by the spot, all three saw the luminous figure. This time, both Ivanka and Mirjana recognized her to be the Virgin Mary. Milka, too, believed she was seeing the Madonna. Now the vision was carrying an infant in her arms. The girls were both joyful and afraid at the same time. Mirjana and Ivanka had left a note for their friend Vicka to come and join them after Vicka finished some work. When Vicka joined up with them at Podbrdo, Mirjana said to her,

"Look up there, Our Lady!"

"What do you mean, Our Lady? What is the matter with you?" Vicka replied.

Frightened, Vicka ran away, and while she was on her way home, she ran into twenty-year-old Ivan Ivanković and sixteen-year-old Ivan Dragićević. They were picking apples.

"Ivan," Vicka said to the younger Ivan, "they said Our Lady has appeared up there. Let us go there, you and me. I am afraid."

"Of course we'll go, but why are you afraid?" he replied. Vicka joined the younger and older Ivan and they went to the hill. Once there, Vicka again spoke to Ivan Dragićević.

"Do you see anything?"

Ivan was nowhere to be found. Afraid, he ran away and dropped all his apples. The older Ivan (Ivanković) remained and said, "I see something completely white, turning."

Milka exclaimed, "I see the Madonna!" From the next day forward, Milka and the older Ivan (Ivanković) would need to go by faith alone since they would not see the vision again after that first day. Vicka saw dark hair and a gown on what appeared to be a beautiful lady. She saw the lady covering and uncovering an infant several times.

The vision appeared to be waving her hand, beckoning them to come closer. They recognized that she was calling them closer, but nobody dared to go up. Instead, they left since neither of them was ready to take that step. Vicka left first and then the others also went home. When they arrived, they told relatives about who they saw. They were teased for doing so.

"You should have caught her," Milka's uncle said.

That concludes the first day. Six people saw the luminous vision, but only four of these would see her again. She didn't speak any words that day, but she was clearly seen and was described as a beautiful lady. Mirjana was asked how she knew it was the Blessed Virgin. She replied, "My whole being knew without a doubt that this lady of unexplainable beauty was the Mother of God." Mirjana, Ivanka, Vicka, and Ivan Dragićević would return to the same place the next day. The twenty-year-old Ivan Ivanković didn't want to return, and reportedly, Milka didn't have permission to go this time. She was asked by her mother to take care of the sheep. However, Milka's sixteen-year-old sister Marija Pavlović went instead. Marija asked Vicka if she would come and get her and ten-year-old Jakov Čolo if the lady appeared again. [19]

Ivanka Ivanković—Elez at Beginning of Apparitions (Left) and Today (Right)

Ivanka Ivanković—Elez was born on June 21, 1966, in Bijakovici, in the parish of Medjugorje. She was the first one who saw Our Lady. She had daily apparitions until May 7, 1985. On that day, confiding to her the tenth secret, Our Lady told her that for the rest of her life, she would have one yearly apparition on June 25, the anniversary of the apparitions. Ivanka is married, she has three children, and she lives with her family in Medjugorje. The prayer intention that Our Lady confided in her: for families.

The Second Day, June 25, 1981

(Refer to endnote twenty to make reference to sources for information and quotations used concerning the second day of the visions, June 25, 1981).

The following day at about the same time (6:00 p.m.), the lady appeared again in the same location on the hill, about two hundred meters up (roughly 650 feet). Mirjana, Ivanka, and Vicka were again at the base of the hill and looking up to the vision. As she did the previous day, Ivanka saw the lady first.

"Look, the Madonna!" she said to the others, pointing in the direction of the vision.

Right away, Vicka said she recognized her hair, gown, eyes, and face. As she'd promised, Vicka then went to go and get Marija Pavlović and Jakov Čolo. When they arrived, the lady again motioned with her hand to invite the children to come and draw closer. This time, they moved ahead to begin the climb upward toward the spot where she was. According to curious eyewitnesses who followed behind them, they moved up the hill at an unusually fast speed. They were actually running over rocks and thorn bushes. Mirjana's uncle was one of those who witnessed this. He said that it takes "at least twelve minutes to get up there," and that the youngsters "did it in just two." Seeing that, he said it scared him to death. When they arrived close to the vision, they were completely unscathed with not a mark on them according to eyewitnesses. There, they met up with sixteen-year-old Ivan Dragićević. He had come from another direction and had climbed up with some friends. Ivan wanted to redeem himself from the previous day when he ran away and dropped all his apples. He would do much more than that.

One of the most significant things that took place during the apparition of June 25 was that the young people had formed the group of six to whom the Virgin Mary would reportedly appear for years to come. Also of much significance was that this was the first day the children actually reported to speak with the Madonna. After being strangely brought to their knees when getting to within about seven feet of the vision, Ivanka spoke first. She asked about her mother who had just died two months earlier. The reply was that her mother is "well," was "with her in heaven," and that she "should not worry." Mirjana said to the vision that the people will think they are crazy for talking about this and that they won't believe them.

According to the seers, Mary just smiled. The vision was reported to last about ten to fifteen minutes. At the end, the Virgin was seen hovering in the air and the visionaries didn't know what to say. As she left, the lady said, "Go in God's peace." The children were still somewhat frightened and kind of overwhelmed by this experience. Ivanka, in particular, was very emotional and sobbed all the way down the mountain. Marinko Ivanković, a man of about forty who lived across the street from Marija Pavlović, tried to talk to and help the children after they returned home. Skeptical at first, he later believed them after hearing their story. [20]

Ivan Dragićević in Two Early Photos From the 1980's (Left and Right). Just below these two images is a more recent picture of Ivan

Ivan Dragićević was born on May 25, 1965 in Bijakovici, in the parish of Medjugorje. He still has daily apparitions. Our Lady entrusted nine secrets to him. Ivan is married and he has four children. With his family, he lives in the USA and in Medjugorje. The prayer intention that Our Lady confided in him: for young people and for priests.

The Third Day, June 26, 1981

(Refer to endnote twenty-two to make reference to sources for information and quotations used concerning the third day of the visions, June 26, 1981).

Word had spread throughout Medjugorje and the surrounding towns that the Holy Mother was appearing, and a crowd of some three thousand gathered to be present with the children on the hill that day. Marinko Ivanković accompanied the six seers as they went to the place where they'd seen the Virgin the previous day. He had taken on the role of an adult guardian angel and wanted to protect the children. He brought holy water with him. This time, three lights flashed before the lady appeared. Marinko encouraged Vicka to sprinkle the vision with holy water. Vicka came up close and sprinkled the whole bottle on the vision, saying, "If you are the Virgin, stay with us. If you are not, depart from us." The vision reportedly smiled and was pleased by the gesture. Then the children began to ask her some questions. Marinko encouraged Ivanka to ask the lady why she had come. Her response was, "I have come because there are many true believers here. I wish to be with you to convert and to reconcile the whole world."

Since Ivanka's mother was alone when she died at the hospital, Ivanka inquired whether she had left any message for her. The lady's reply was, "Obey your grandmother and help her because she is old."

Mirjana asked the lady who she was. She said, "I am the Blessed Virgin Mary."

They asked her for a sign so that the people would believe them. Our Lady replied, quoting her Son's words from the Bible (Gospel of John 20:29).[21] "Blessed are those who have not seen and who believe."

The children asked her why she chose them to appear to because they thought of themselves as quite ordinary. "Why are you appearing to us? We are no better than others," they said.

"I do not necessarily choose the best," was the lady's reply.

The vision was much longer than the previous two, going for about a half hour, and it was higher up on the hill. The lady promised to appear again the following day in the place she appeared the day before.

Afterward, the lady appeared again but to Marija alone. According to eyewitnesses, Marija had mysteriously been pushed aside on the way down the hill by a strange force and was brought to her knees. For about ten minutes, she stayed with the lady. Marija said Mary appeared before a bare wooden cross, and the Virgin was crying. Her words given through Marija were, "Peace, peace, peace. Be reconciled. Only peace. Make peace with God and among yourselves. For that it is necessary to believe, to pray, to fast, and to go to confession." Marija later spoke of this: "It was an overwhelming experience. I saw the Madonna weeping, and the sight drove me to commit totally to her request. She had come to inspire all of us to search for peace—peace in our own hearts, peace in our families, peace in the world." [22]

Marija Pavlović-Lunetti in 1980's (left) and Today (right)

Marija Pavlović-Lunetti was born on April 1, 1965, in Bijakovici, in the parish of Medjugorje. She still has daily apparitions. Through her, Our Lady gives her message to the parish and the world. From March 1, 1984, to January 8, 1987, the message was given every Thursday and, since January 1987, every twenty-fifth of the month. Our Lady entrusted nine secrets to her. Marija is married and she has four children. With her family, she lives in Italy and in Medjugorje. The prayer intention that Our Lady confided in her: for the souls in purgatory.

Day Four, June 27, 1981, Onward

And thus, it had begun—the first three days. I wanted to provide a detailed account of what happened from the very beginning because I think it's both interesting and important to see how this all came together in the first place and to hear of the various human reactions of the six children to this astonishing new event in their lives. The lady would continue to appear to the six young people each evening around the six o'clock hour in Medjugorje. She would appear to each one of them *every day* until December

12

25, 1982, at which point Mirjana ceased to have daily visions. From that point forward, Mirjana would see the Madonna only once a year, and the other five would continue to have daily visions.

At the time this book was written, Ivan, Marija, and Vicka continued to report (with very few exceptions) a daily vision of the Madonna from June 25, 1981, until now. The other three, Mirjana, Ivanka, and Jakov have each ceased having daily visions. Each report a vision from the Madonna once annually now while Mirjana also reports an inner voice of Mary, called a locution, on the second of every month. This is sometimes accompanied by a vision. I've been with Mirjana for about six of these experiences, which she has on the second of each month in Medjugorje. Each time I was there, she reported a vision, and she was accompanied by a large crowd. I've always found the experience peaceful. It looks like she is having an otherworldly experience, sometimes appearing very emotional and at other times, deeply prayerful. Our Lady gives Mirjana a message, and then the message is announced over a loudspeaker in several different languages. Mirjana's annual apparition is on her birthday, March 18. Ivanka sees her on the recognized anniversary of the visions, June 25 of every year, and Jakov has an annual Christmas Day apparition from the Blessed Virgin.

Positive Views of Theologians

The astounding number of visions and messages to these six individuals makes many wonder about the meaning of the event. "Never in the history of Christianity has the Blessed Virgin Mary appeared to so many people over so long a period of time with such regularity. Moreover, it seems that the apparitions at Medjugorje have ushered in a new Marian age" (Rev. Robert Faricy, SJ).[23] Medjugorje also had the support of the renowned Catholic theologian Cardinal Hans Urs von Balthasar (1905-1988). "Medjugorje's theology," he said, "rings true. I am convinced of its truth. And everything is authentic in a Catholic sense. What is happening there is so evident, so convincing."[24] Father Faricy also recognized, "God has sent Mary, the Mother of Jesus, to call us to repent and turn to him, and to receive the Lord's love in our life. That is at the center."[25] Fr. Rene Laurentin, in his book *Is the Virgin Mary Appearing at Medjugorje?*, also cites the following theologians in support of Medjugorje (positions or titles may have changed since Laurentin's book was published):

- Father Michael Scanlon, President of the University of Steubenville, Ohio;

- Father John Bertolucci of the same university

- Father Beck of Milan, born at Zagreb, director of a retreat house in Milan. He has visited Medjugorje three times

- Father Thomas Forrest, who spent two days at Medjugorje

- Father Tomislav Ivancic, professor of fundamental theology at Zagreb, who also spent two days at Medjugorje

- Father A. Dongo, Belgian theologian

- Father Radogost Grafenauer, SJ, consulted by the bishop of Mostar because of his prudent and critical outlook, has become strongly in favor of the apparitions. "All these in different degrees exclude a purely natural explanation and, even more, a diabolical influence." (ref. note #139).

Based on parish accounting, over 28 million people have taken Communion (called "hosts") in Medjugorje since 1985 when they first began to compile statistics. The news agency *Reuters* estimated that the events at Medjugorje "have now drawn more than 30 million pilgrims" (www. reuters.com, "Vatican Probes Claims of Apparitions at Medjugorje," 3/17/2010).[26] For the ten-year period of 2002-2011, parish statistics account that an average of 32,193 priests concelebrated Mass in Medjugorje *each of those years*.[27] It's likely that the number of people who've reported Christian conversion after having traveled there is in the millions. I can't prove that figure or provide an endnote for the conversion of hearts. The witnesses speak for themselves. Most of us know at least one person who reported Christian conversion or other graces through Medjugorje. I count myself among those who have been thus affected through my involvements with this ongoing phenomenon. I know a number of others.

Mirjana Dragićević-Soldo in the 1980's (Top Picture). Two More Recent Pictures of Mirjana Today, Side-by-Side (Below)

Mirjana Dragićević-Soldo was born on March 18, 1965, in Sarajevo. She had daily apparitions until December 25, 1982. On that day, entrusting to her the tenth secret, Our Lady told her that for the rest of her life she would have one yearly apparition, on March 18. Since August 2, 1987, on each second day of the month, she hears interiorly Our Lady's voice and prays with her for unbelievers. Sometimes she also sees her. Mirjana is married, she has two children, and she lives with her family in Medjugorje. The prayer intention that Our Lady confided in her: for unbelievers, those who have not come to know the love of God.

Mary and MTV

The popular music-video TV cable broadcast, called MTV, launched the same year-1981- that the Madonna first appeared in Medjugorje. Ironically, it was during the 80's that we also witnessed rising popularity of the singer, "Madonna." So in this age, if someone says Madonna, they may have to clarify who they're referring to. Do they mean the pop music idol or do they mean the holy Mother of God? During these thirty-one years, the Holy Mother has faced much competition. This has been not just for her name, but for her message. She competes with the many modern-day instruments of entertainment and communication—MTV, cell phones, laptops, internet, iPods, TVs, iPads, DVDs, MP3 players, and all other modern gadgets of our tech-savvy world. These help us to meet human needs and provide good and useful purposes. I'm not putting them down and I use some of these regularly. Mary does not identify these media or communication devices as bad or evil. At the same time, she recommends turning off the TV, for example. Too much of these things distract us from the spiritual life, sometimes lead us astray, or may send a message that is far different from the one that Mary teaches. Secular media today frequently reinforces attachment to the world, the material, and to things of the flesh. In the 1980s hit song, Madonna sang these lyrics: "This is a material world and I am a material girl." When the Virgin Mary came upon the scene in 1981, she had her work cut out for her. Madonna's lyrics spoke to a culture focused heavily on material things. The '80s movie *Wall Street* had actor Michael Douglas teaching new hire Charlie Sheen that "greed is good." In contrast, the heavenly Madonna teaches detachment from the world and asks us to consider higher realms.

The Blessed Virgin has seen many lost souls become prodigal sons and daughters who don't know Jesus or the truth that he taught. She speaks also to those who go to church but for some reason are not happy or have little peace. The following words that she related to the visionaries are significant: "There is only one God and only one mediator, Jesus Christ."[28] Based on these and other reported messages passed to us from the visionaries, I've concluded that Medjugorje has a Christ-centered intention and focus. She's developed a school of prayer in this place and has repeatedly recommended daily Bible reading. She encourages us to pray often and to develop the discipline to pray every day.

The visits to Medjugorje were not the first time that the Virgin Mary has been reported to appear on earth to human instruments. Her intentions, motives, and desires, as related by the Medjugorje visionaries, are very similar to those from previous apparitions in history. She emphasized prayer, penance, and repentance when she appeared to fourteen-year-old Bernadette Soubirous in Lourdes, France, in 1858. She disclosed numerous other revelations to three shepherd children in Fatima, Portugal, in 1917, including the prediction of a second world war if her messages were not heeded enough. After thorough investigations, the Catholic Church approved and expressed belief in Mary's appearances in both Lourdes and Fatima. Through revelations like those in Lourdes, Fatima, and (I believe) Medjugorje, she tries to draw us into the spiritual life and become closer to God. She helps and encourages us to advance against sinful ways and reject temptations. Her messages are timely advice based on the circumstances of the time and the people she speaks to. She does all God permits her in order to save the lost from further problems in this life or to face perdition in the hereafter.

Despite all the good fruits that are related to the Medjugorje phenomenon, certain priests and others struggle with it for these reasons:

1. The sheer number of reported visions is unprecedented and very unusual (exceeding eleven thousand by 2006).[29]

2. These private revelations have taken place over such a long time period (the thirty-first anniversary was June 25, 2012). She only appeared eighteen times in Lourdes to Bernadette and once a month for six months to the Fatima seers Jacinta, Francesco, and Lucia.

3. The fact the Great Sign (a physical miracle promised by Mary on Apparition Hill a.k.a. Podbrdo) has not yet come.

I acknowledge all objections that I've heard. I've not exactly received a Justin Bieber-like fan reaction while trying to put this message forward. Sometimes, I get blank stares. Other times, I get questions like, "What does the church have to say about it?" or "Is it safe over there?" Others have said, "Yeah, my mom went there." I've also spoken with many who share my outlook on this. They're positive, believing, and don't view it as insignificant. Many such people believe Mother Mary is working out a plan and that we've not seen the end of it. I know this phenomenon is unusual and unprecedented. "Don't shoot the messenger." Let's try to comprehend the meaning of the event in a positive way and consider what positive effects these events have had on the lives of many.

Vicka Ivanković—Mijatovic in Early 1980s (Left) and Today (Right)

Vicka Ivanković—Mijatovic was born on September 9, 1964, in Bijakovici, in the parish of Medjugorje. She still has daily apparitions. Our Lady entrusted nine secrets to her. Vicka is married, has two children, and lives in Krehin Gradac, near Medjugorje. The prayer intention that Our Lady confided in her: for the sick.

From the Bishop's Office

In the two indented paragraphs (just below) are the words of the bishop in the diocese of the Medjugorje region when Mary reportedly began appearing. I'm referring to the late bishop Pavao Žanić (1918-2000). In mid-August 1981, he comments on reports of the still-new apparitions. As you can read, the bishop was actually supportive of the visionaries in the beginning.

> The public expects us to say something about the events
> in the parish of Medjugorje, where six children claim
> the Madonna appears to them . . . It is certain that the

children have not been "talked into" anything and have not—certainly not by the Church—been encouraged to speak falsehoods. Everything indicates that the children are not lying . . . When the Jews tried to silence the Apostles, according to the Acts of the Apostles, a teacher of the law, highly regarded by all the people, Gamiliel, said to the Jewish assembly:

"If their purpose or activity is human in its origins, they will destroy themselves. If on the other hand, what they say comes from God, you will not be able to destroy them. You might even be found opposing God!" (Acts 5:38-39;[30] Monsignor Pavao Žanić, bishop of Mostar-Duvno, per the publication *Glas Koncila*, August 16, 1981)

Within a short time later, the bishop became negative about the apparitions and eventually became a strong adversary of the six visionaries. It requires some explanation to understand why the bishop turned, but I believe at least some of the reasons are detailed in chapter 11. Here, there's documentation that the bishop faced pressure from both the Communist government and some of his own diocesan clergy not to be supportive of the apparitions or visionaries. Also, he was probably scandalized in finding out through Vicka's diary that the Virgin said two Franciscan priests, defrocked from the priesthood, were "not guilty."[31] Likely, Žanić was irate because he supported the case for their removal.

I need not add anything to what Monsignor Žanić said that day in August 1981. If you relate his comments to subsequent events, it appears he was prophetic. In those days, if someone was talking about an apparition, I probably would have shied away from the conversation and thought they were talking about a ghost. If someone tried to bring up the subject of Medjugorje, I would have said, "Medju-what?" I did not yet keep a rosary in my pocket, and I only thought to say one if I had a serious problem or an urgent need. I went to Sunday Mass, but I sat on the back stairway in the vestibule with my friends. Other than Mass, I wasn't that involved with the church. As for what I wanted to be, I wanted to be successful in business and hopefully make a lot of money. Even by 1988 when I first traveled to Medjugorje, the priesthood hadn't crossed my mind. After college graduation and four years in the accounting field, I decided to apply to a Catholic seminary. I studied for five years at the seminary and was ordained a priest at the end of the five-year formation. There's more to say about why I made such a change in my life, but that's better explained in the next chapter.

Pictured below between Vicka (far left) and Ivanka (third from left), the head of ten-year-old visionary Jakov Čolo barely makes it above the altar before which the visionaries kneel during an early apparition. Upon his first vision of the Madonna, Jakov said, "Now when I have seen her, I can die. I don't mind." In the earlier years, the presence of the fidgety young boy was noteworthy in terms of strengthening belief in the apparitions.

Also pictured are Mirjana, Marija, and Ivan (fourth, fifth, and sixth from left)

Jakov Čolo at Beginning of Apparitions (Left) and Today (Right)

Jakov Čolo was born on March 6, 1971, in Sarajevo. He had daily apparitions from June 25, 1981, to September 12, 1998. On that day, entrusting to him the tenth secret, Our Lady told him that for the rest of his life he would have one yearly apparition, on Christmas Day. Jakov is married and he has three children. He lives with his family in Medjugorje. The prayer intention that Our Lady confided in him: for the sick.

Each chapter closes with actual reported words of the Holy Mother. Beginning on January 25, 1987, the Madonna reportedly began giving messages intended for the whole world on the twenty-fifth of every month. The messages communicated on the twenty-fifth are given through the visionary Marija Pavlović-Lunetti and almost always begin with the words, "Dear children . . ."

> Dear children, today again I am calling you to prayer and complete surrender to God. You know that I love you and am coming here out of love, so that I could show you the path of peace and salvation for your souls. I want you to listen to me and not permit Satan to seduce you. Dear children, Satan is strong enough! Therefore, I ask you to dedicate your prayers to me so that those who are under his influence may be saved. Give witness by your life, sacrifice your lives for the salvation of the

world. I am with you and I am grateful to you, but in Heaven you shall receive the Father's reward which he has promised you. Therefore, little children, do not be afraid. If you pray, Satan cannot injure you even a little, because you are God's children and He is watching over you. Pray, and let the rosary always be in your hands as a sign to Satan that you belong to me. Thank you for having responded to my call. (February 25, 1988, reportedly from the Virgin Mary)[32]

Chapter 2

Called to Conversion

This chapter focuses on the early influence of a 1988 pilgrimage to Medjugorje, my first visit to this town. I name the chapter "Called to Conversion" because I was thus called from this place. Like everyone, I struggled with sin but was invited to explore how I might change or improve in the context of my life of faith. Present to celebrate the seventh anniversary of the apparitions, this was the first time I'd stepped into Balkan or Communist territory. It was also the first time I'd walked into a town where they said the Mother of God was presently appearing. My dad had made a private pilgrimage to the same place six months previously. Since he liked what he experienced, he invited my sister and me to join him for a summer pilgrimage there the last week of June 1988.

It was a difficult time personally, and I was in a bad mood during the first couple days of the weeklong pilgrimage. One of my first experiences in Medjugorje was a conversation with my dad in our hotel room. He asked me if I was okay. In response, I said I felt kind of down. He asked me if I knew what that was about. I knew the reason, and I talked about the frustration I was experiencing with choosing public accounting as a career. I also had some dejected feelings about just having been laid off from my first big job out of college as an auditor. Shortly after college graduation, I worked just under a year at a very large public accounting firm in Boston.

Two weeks prior to our scheduled departure for Medjugorje, the managing director of the firm asked me and about twelve others to pack our audit bags and leave. Though I was relieved in some ways to be out of the position, I was now unemployed and didn't know what else to do. After majoring in accounting at a business college, I found out that I didn't like auditing people's books at all. I was afraid to seek another public accounting job because I so disliked the first. In what seemed like a leap, my dad warned me about how Satan likes to discourage, trip us up, and make us lose hope. He said he thought the devil was working on me and encouraged me to come closer to the Virgin Mary while I was there. He advised me to tell her what troubled me and simply be open with her. It seemed like good advice. At the same time, I'd not been thinking along the lines of *Satan* simply because I was down. I didn't contend the point though, thinking perhaps that he could have been right. As advised, I accepted Dad's advice and tried to talk to and get closer to Mary during the weeklong trip. I shared with Mother Mary my troubles and asked for her assistance. I also began praying a daily rosary while I was there. Many Catholics and some non-Catholics pray the rosary, using a set of beads to count the prayers. The rosary is intended as a devotion to the Virgin Mary, but it's also meant to be a meditation on the mysteries of Christ's life. Up to this point, I would have said a rosary only upon my dad's direction or in a rough or desperate moment. I received a grace there to say at least five decades of the rosary every day. Appendix 4 provides much more information about the rosary.

First Encounter with the Visionary Vicka Ivanković—Mijatovic

Within a day or two after the talk with dad in the hotel room, I came upon a simple house on a small road in Medjugorje. On its outdoor stairway, the visionary Vicka Ivanković was speaking to pilgrims. She's now Vicka Ivanković—Mijatovic and claims to have had daily visions of the Mother of Jesus for thirty-one years in Medjugorje. I've believed her since that first day I saw her speak in 1988. At this point, Vicka was twenty-three and claimed to have seen the Madonna for seven years. She's charismatic, open with people, and friendly. For this reason, she's probably one of the most popular of the six visionaries. The picture below is where I originally saw Vicka, and this is where she usually speaks to pilgrims.

Vicka Ivanković—Mijatovic Speaking to Pilgrims in Medjugorje

She addresses one language group after another. An interpreter is present to translate the message into the language of whichever group is there. Vicka explains to the many pilgrims the content and meaning of the Virgin Mary's messages. As I looked at her this summer day in '88, she appeared completely sincere and really seemed to be speaking from her heart. She communicated in her expressions enthusiasm, confidence, and peace. I found Vicka very convincing, and her talk was one of the major reasons I began to believe in the visions. At present, Vicka lives just outside Medjugorje with her husband and two children. Their house is modest, and they live a simple family life.

Pray with the Heart

During Vicka's talk, the message "pray with the heart" stands out in my memory. Through the visionaries, Mary has guided us to communicate with her and with Jesus from the heart and not just with rote prayers. She invites us to a conversation with her and with her Son. Prayer with the heart requires that we be in touch with our emotions and spiritual life. It requires "getting out of our heads," being real, and praying from the center of our souls. As an example, someone might say, "Lord, I'm afraid" or "Mary, I'm worried and confused. I don't know what to do." Sometimes in repentance, I'll use the words, "Jesus, forgive me. I'm sorry for my sins. Help me to do better." Conversations like this build friendship, relationship, and trust. For these to grow, we must set aside time for God or the Holy Mother in order to build the relationship. What kind of relationship or friendship could we build with someone if we didn't communicate? It wouldn't get very far, would it? For most people, talking to God is easier, and listening is more difficult. As we listen, God will sometimes communicate a message back, but not always. When God communicates something back, he usually does this by speaking to our hearts and if we can listen and quiet ourselves long enough, we can perceive the message. His words are often accompanied by peace and that's a way to know it's from him. In talking with the Madonna, Mary said to me at times, "I am with you" or "Do not be afraid." If you're fortunate and pray well, you may even receive specific guidance, such as "Go here" (specified to place) or "Don't go there." They may say, "Do this (action specified)" or "Don't do that." With less significant decisions, they may be silent on a course of action and let you exercise your own judgment.

In a typical spiritual journey, we'll have times when we can hear heaven really well. At other times, we'll have dry spells when all we want is a word from God, but we can't recognize a single one. There's times when we may have absolutely no idea what God is trying to say to us. He may be speaking or he may be silent. If we can't comprehend what God is communicating, we may not be in a place psychologically or spiritually where we can hear him. When we can hear God, he usually sends signals subtly. It's more likely to hear him in the midst of silence than in some loud or explicit revelation. Prayer is a gift of God's grace, and I've learned that I really can't make anything happen. I just have to be open to whatever grace is offered. The best we can do is give time and effort, pray with the heart, and be open to how grace works in the experience. If you have trouble focusing, you could try using a journal or Bible. For me, it helps to start off with a rosary, a passage from the Bible, or by saying some rote prayers. Then I may transition to a conversation once I'm settled. Prayer is different for each person, so I can't say there's any one way to pray. It does appear from Vicka's testimony, however, that more prayer from the heart is recommended in particular. Vicka said that, like flowers need water, we need prayer. If we don't water the flowers, they will wither and die. If we water them though, they blossom and become beautiful.

Materialism

A second message Vicka gave during that same talk concerned the dangers of materialism. That concerned me because I'd set my heart on making a lot of money. Now what? Was I supposed to not want that? I went to a business school (Babson College) and had learned much about finance and how to succeed in business and make money. Was I supposed to just throw this all away now? No, that's not what this meant. At the same time, I needed to hear this warning about materialism. It's not such a simple issue to negotiate. Since it's an important issue that requires a lengthier explanation, I devoted chapter 7 to doing just that. This paragraph begins to identify the problem. In general, many people make too much of things. A priest friend of mine, Father Tom, preached one day that we'd even become the "Kingdom of Thingdom." This tends to be a more serious problem in affluent countries simply because we have so much stuff. The more money or stuff one has, sometimes there's a greater risk to be more devoted to the material than is healthy. In one radical message from Medjugorje, Mary said: "The West has made civilization progress, but without God, as if they were their own creators" (ref. note 104). Of course, Mary's not speaking of everyone, and she knows that many have their hearts in the right place. Nonetheless, from what she's revealed, there's also many whose hearts have drifted far away from God.

Sometimes, the visionaries travel. Ivan Dragićević spoke on April 8, 2006, while in the USA. Right after the time of his daily apparition, Ivan revealed these words of Our Lady while speaking at St. Joseph's Church in Wakefield, Massachusetts: "My dear children, today, more than ever before, this world builds toward its major crisis. But, my dear children, the greatest crisis of all is the crisis of faith in God because you have abandoned him. My dear children, this world, this mankind, your families have started to move toward the future without God." [33] Again, she is not speaking of everyone. At the same time, she's giving a warning to those who've become so preoccupied with this world that God has become an afterthought.

The Rosary

Vicka also disclosed in that talk Mary's recommendation to pray the rosary and to use the rosary to protect oneself against the devil. The devil? Many churches hardly even mention the devil anymore. He's often dismissed as a superstitious wonder, a carryover from overzealous or simplistic thought of the Middle Ages. Our Lady of Medjugorje disagrees. The Mother of God does not dismiss the attacks of the devil at all and refers to this difficult reality many times at Medjugorje. For me, I've come to see that the power of the devil is real, and he can create havoc in our lives if we let him. He tries to discourage and mislead everyone but especially preys on weaker people who are more vulnerable to attacks, temptation, or negative thinking. He also likes to go after priests. He knows each person's weakness, and he'll try to hit us in our Achilles' heel. We must fight against the devil's tactics, and the Virgin teaches that one of our most powerful weapons is prayer.

The Madonna's exhortation to pray the rosary is not new. She gave the same message at Fatima, Portugal, through three shepherd children in 1917—Jacinta, Francesco, and Lucia. In Medjugorje though, she's asked for fifteen decades of the rosary each day! I can't say I've done that. Sometimes, I say five decades and on others I say ten. I've found the rosary very beneficial in my own faith walk. With instructions and a set of rosary beads, you can teach yourself. If you don't have beads, you can count Hail Marys using your ten fingers. I now keep a rosary in my pocket almost all the time. A diagram of a typical rosary is included for your reference in Appendix 4, along with text for all the prayers and instructions.

Heaven, Hell, and Purgatory

The last topic I remember Vicka addressing was that the Virgin Mary had shown her heaven, hell, and purgatory. Since I already believed in each of these places, I wasn't surprised by these revelations. Still, it was good for me to have it confirmed. In appendix 1, there is a vivid description of what Vicka saw in purgatory and hell. Also in the appendix are statements of the visionary Jakov about his sight of heaven, hell, and purgatory. They both reported being taken to these places by Our Lady of Medjugorje during the first year of the visions in 1981.

When my conversion began here in 1988, I needed to hear each of the four themes Vicka mentioned: (1) recommendation to pray with the heart, (2) the problem of materialism (putting things and money before God or in place of God), (3) recommendation to pray the rosary, and (4) the confirmation and description of heaven, hell, and purgatory.

Prayer Groups

In addition to individual prayer, Mary has strongly recommended the formation of prayer groups. Hundreds of prayer groups have since formed in the USA at the recommendation of Our Lady of Medjugorje. I'm sure there're many others abroad. Of the prayer meetings in which I have taken part recently, I have found that the most powerful or anointed ones are those that use musical accompaniment. The use of keyboards, guitars, drums, flutes, horns, and the like strengthen the worship and offer a unique form of praise. Worship such as this is favorable to God, and we're instructed to do so in the Bible. Consider these words from Psalm 150: "Give praise with blasts upon the horn. Praise Him with harp and lyre. Give praise with tambourines and dance, praise Him with flutes and strings. Give praise with crashing cymbals, praise Him with sounding cymbals. Let everything that has breathe give praise to the Lord."[34] Psalm 98 is similar: "Shout with joy to the Lord, all the earth; break into song; sing praise. Sing praise to the Lord with the harp, with the harp and melodious song. With trumpets and the sound of the horn, shout with joy to the King, the Lord."[35]

Before and After

Conversion will be mentioned numerous times in the book since it's one of the five key themes of the Virgin's call. In this context, conversion is about our interior since it begins with changes in our heart. When that change takes place, it's later reflected by the way we live our life. If we're experiencing conversion, we'll gradually be overcoming sin and increasing in virtue. As for me, I was a sinner before I went over to Medjugorje and remained a sinner afterward, as I still am today. I became, however, a sinner who prayed and was better able to accept the call to conversion in my life. I chose to take the steps that the church calls us all to take—by changing my ways and by improving my relationship with God and with man. Accepting the Virgin's recommendation, I also began a monthly confession and received Communion more frequently by going to Mass more often. With the rest of humanity, I will still, nonetheless, continue to need change and improve upon imperfections for my whole life.

I'll close this chapter by noting that I left Medjugorje that last week of June 1988 with a sense of peace. I had completed my first pilgrimage to this holy place. It was a peace that stayed with me for a good while. I had a mysterious calm replace my down feelings about my future and professional career. I now had this optimistic sense that everything would turn out fine. And it did. I still had no intention to study for the priesthood. Those thoughts would not begin to emerge until about a year after coming home from this trip. No, when I returned home, it was time to pound the pavement to find my next job. I didn't have it so bad that summer. I had some money from severance pay. So I spent a good number of days at the beach with a friend in between job interviews. I decided to try another public accounting firm. This time, I sought a smaller firm with less auditing. By late August, I received an offer as a staff accountant from another company in the Boston area. I was back to the desk, the pencils, and the adding machine. I still had to balance a lot of balance sheets and tally many numbers. In the spring, I'd be up to my neck in tax returns. The audits were fewer and easier because they were with smaller companies with less complex systems. I liked the people I worked with, and the job turned out much better. I also began to experience changes in my spiritual life. As I tried to live out the message of Our Lady of Medjugorje, I began to cultivate more peace and stronger faith in God. The message she's given is an accentuated part of the Gospel that's meant for our times. For the sake of brevity, I'll just name the five themes now. They are prayer, conversion, faith, fasting, and peace.

You know, dear children, that God grants special graces in prayer. Therefore, seek and pray in order that you may be able to comprehend all that I am giving here. I call you, dear children, to pray with the heart. You know that without prayer you cannot comprehend all that God is planning through each one of you. Therefore, pray! I desire that through each one of you God's plan may be fulfilled, that all which God has planted in your heart may keep on growing. So pray that God's blessing may protect each one of you from all the evil that is threatening you. I bless you, dear children. Thank you for having responded to my call. (The Blessed Virgin Mary, message to the world through the visionary Marija Pavlović-Lunetti, April 25, 1987)[36]

Chapter 3

Healings, Signs, and Wonders

I decided to return to Medjugorje for the second time during the fall of 1990. I had an important decision to make, and also, I was still very curious about what was going on there. So there were two motives to go back—to help me make decisions and also to have the chance to spend more time with the Madonna while I believed that she continued to appear in the Medjugorje region. I believe the Virgin Mother was beckoning me to go back. I named this chapter as I did because I saw signs and wonders during that trip, which I cannot explain using reason alone. Those incidents and signs will be explained in this chapter. My dad also wanted to go back, so we decided to make the pilgrimage together. Dad witnessed three of the signs along with me. The healings of which I write about concern others. These were physical diseases of people who either traveled to Medjugorje, who were prayed for by someone there, or who simply read about the Medjugorje messages and acted upon them while at home.

Regarding my work, I was at the new accounting firm for two years by the time I made this second pilgrimage. Though the second accounting job was much better than the first, I was still questioning whether I wanted to continue in this profession. Whereas I felt lost at the large firm, the atmosphere at the new company was much different and better for me. There was far more of a family atmosphere, and there were only about eight employees plus the tax partner and the audit partner. Auditing was only about 25 percent of my work there in comparison with 100 percent at the first firm. In addition to audits, I did compilations, reviews, and a large number of tax returns. Compilations and reviews could be described as lower-grade audits. I liked providing these services much better than audits because I could apply more of my basic accounting skills, and there was not so much work testing the client's accounting system. As such, there were fewer inquiries of personnel and tests of internal controls as required by full audits. In some compilations, I could actually create the balance sheet and income statement for the client, relying on the financial records they provided. In audits, the financial statements were already completed when we arrived at the client's office. Our job was to do many tests and to make a statement at the end of our examination to express an opinion as to whether the financial statements were considered free of material error.

Accounts of Physical Healing

I'd like to express an opinion on a different matter now. I believe there's a direct relationship between the healing of numerous physical diseases and the Medjugorje phenomenon. I hope you'll agree that this statement is free of material error. As I invited you in the introduction, you can be the jury and make that judgment for yourselves. Before witnessing to the signs and wonders I saw in 1990, I'd like to summarize several Medjugorje healing stories. I'm not sure the physical healings I account for in this section can be audited quite as scientifically as the accounting data I once examined. The Catholic Church, on the other hand, will require the healings to be proven if they're accepted as evidence in support of the authenticity of the Medjugorje apparitions. There's a substantial amount of public information available now that demonstrate that a significant number of people report being healed in relation to their Medjugorje experiences. Numerous doctors of the same patients back them up with respect to their remarkable recoveries. These appear to be well documented, and the Medjugorje parish, St. James Church, keeps a log of all healings reported along with the related medical records and evidence. A new book by a medical writer says that "more than four hundred healings have been recorded at the apparition site of Medjugorje—from the healing of bone spurs and deafness to cancer remission and recovery from severe brain damage."[37] The book, *A Place of Healing,* by Connecticut medical writer John Dinolfo, documents several dramatic cures, including the case of a boy healed of spina bifada after his grandmother placed a photograph of him on the altar at St. James Church in the remote village. "He leads a normal life and very active life," writes Dinolfo of the boy today, "without symptoms of spina bifada" (a deformity of the spine that can result in extensive neurological disabilities). The figure of four hundred healings represents only those cases logged at the (Medjugorje) parish. Many others have gone unreported. [38]

More recent accounts indicate that the number of documented healings logged at the Medjugorje parish since the apparitions began has increased to at least 532. During 2011, new statistics accompanied the thirty-year anniversary of the Madonna's reported visions. "Key statistics . . . are revealing a parish not quite like most other parishes about the size of four thousand parishioners . . . five hundred thirty-two healings were medically documented. This information was first presented by a Franciscan priest speaking at a Marian Conference in Irvine, California, October 21-23, 2011. The numbers are indeed correct as of the thirtieth anniversary according to Medjugorje parish archivist Marija Dugandzic."[39] It was confirmed by CatholicDaily.net that these findings were reported by a priest to those gathered at the Irvine conference. They identify him as Father Joseph Grbes. He currently serves as pastor at St. Jerome's Croatian Catholic Church in Chicago. [40]

Dinolfo does not pretend to convey that the documented healings related to the Medjugorje experiences have reached the status of fully authenticated miracles by the Catholic Church. In his words, "such cases are often crucial to the final acceptance of an apparition . . . if at least some of them are one day established as officially 'miraculous,' [this] may well figure into the drama of Medjugorje—where controversy still rages over authenticity of the most publicized apparitions since Fatima." [41] In the meantime, we must wait and exercise both reason and faith to conclude whether we believe the Medjugorje cures to be heaven-sent miracles. The healing accounts described in the following paragraphs make reference to specific doctors or hospitals that authenticated the healing of serious sickness. These are referenced in the cases of Megan McMahon, Artie Boyle, and Rita Claus, all from the United States.

The healing of Megan McMahon is also recorded by Dinolfo. At the time, she was a child from Upper Derby, Pennsylvania. McMahon was born with a potentially deadly eye cancer, which is called bilateral retinoblastoma. In 1987, she was taken to Medjugorje. At that time, Megan was three and apparently saw the Virgin herself. Inside St. James Church, "Megan was at one end of the pew, and her mother Jeannie knelt in the center aisle," recounts Dinolfo. As Jeannie continued to pray, she was unaware that the nightly apparition had started in the balcony room. Visionary Marija Pavlović and others were in a room in the balcony. Suddenly, Megan called out, "Mommy, is that the Blessed Mother?" Then Megan, with outstretched arms, began to say loudly in a singsong voice, "I love you, Blessed Mother. I want to kiss and hug you." So striking was the occurrence that those around the girl began to weep. The girl also reported seeing "the big angel" and "three of four baby angels." When the girl recovered from her illness, according to Dinolfo, her surgeon at Philadelphia's Wills Eye Hospital expressed belief that the force of prayer had "definitely" been at work. [42]

Then there is the case of Boston businessman Artie Boyle who was healed of cancer. I've heard Mr. Boyle give witness of the healing while speaking in the Boston area, and I believe very much in its authenticity. The healing was recorded by *ABC News* (ref. note 43): "The Boston man's fight began when he was diagnosed with cancer of the kidney. The situation became desperate when doctors realized the cancer had spread to his lungs. 'When I was rediagnosed, there was a tremendous depression and it felt like a death sentence,' Boyle said on ABC News show *Good Morning America*. Boyle, the father of thirteen children, said he couldn't imagine not being around to coach his kids' hockey games, see their smiles, or grow old with his beloved wife of thirty years. Motivated by faith and a determination to live, Boyle made the journey to Medjugorje . . . a mystical place he had wondered about for many years. Boyle believes the journey there saved his life. 'It was over in Medjugorje where the depression lifted,' he said. 'And I believe I was healed.' When Boyle returned home, a CAT scan showed that one nodule on his lung had disappeared and two others had shrunk to an insignificant size. His physician, Dr. Francis McGovern of Massachusetts General Hospital, says the sudden change was certainly uncommon. 'He has not received any other additional treatment. At this time, we consider him without any evidence of cancer,' McGovern said. Boyle said he believes the spiritual healing he received in Medjugorje allowed for the physical healing. 'I'm not a theologian. I'm not a priest. But I do know that forgiveness and confession are very powerful tools,' he said. 'I'm not sure why I was healed, but I am grateful,' Boyle said. 'Some people are skeptical but all they have to do is look at me. I'm still here'" [43] (article dated November 12, 2004).

The healing of Rita Claus is unique in the respect that the person healed had not traveled to Medjugorje by the time of being healed. Whether she traveled there afterward, I don't know. Rita was from Pittsburgh, Pennsylvania, a teacher and mother of three children, born January 25, 1940. For twenty-six years, she suffered from multiple sclerosis. "She was also one that neither doctors nor medicines were able to help. Reading the book, *Is the Blessed Virgin Appearing in Medjugorje?* (by Laurentin-Rupčić), she decided to accept Our Lady's messages. And once while she was praying the rosary, she felt within herself some unusual warmth. After that, she felt well. And from then until today, the patient is completely well and capable of doing all her domestic and school-related work. There is a solid medical documentation about her sickness and her futile therapy and likewise a professional certification of the doctors on her extraordinary and incomprehensible healing."[44] Another account of Rita's healing records it this way: "Rita Claus, American, married with three daughters; she had multiple sclerosis for twenty-five years, getting about in a wheelchair. In February 1986, she read about Medjugorje and on the evening of 18 June after prayer she knew she must ask for healing. The next day, she could move her feet and legs and by the same evening she ran upstairs, quite recovered."[45]

There are too many healing stories to account for in this chapter, but I want to write briefly about one more. It's the healing of one of the visionaries themselves, Vicka Ivanković—Mijatovic. It's well-known that Vicka suffered from a brain tumor during the earlier years of the apparitions in the 1980s. "She's said to have had a brain tumor that caused severe headaches, coma state periods, nausea, etc., for years. However, on September 25, 1988, the pain stopped. Vicka wrote about her healing seven months *before it happened.*" [46] Recorded below is a letter dated February 4, 1988, which Vicka wrote to Franciscan priest, Father Janko Bubalo:

(from) Bijakovici 4 February 1988

Fr. Janko, That which I promised to you—a ceasing of pains, September 25, 1988. Only under the seal of confession. My greeting to you!

Your little sister, Vicka.[47]

Father Janko wrote the following on the bottom of Vicka's letter:

Received—Fr. Janko Bubalo, 4 February 1988.

"This statement was sealed in an envelope and delivered on February 4, 1988, with the instructions to be opened on September 25, 1988. When the letter was opened, Vicka stopped having pains, just as it was stated in the letter. The president of the new commission studying Medjugorje was present for the letter opening on September 25, 1988 (Bishop Komarica). Vicka's healing has to be of significance in helping prove . . . that the apparitions are indeed real and true. The letter was sealed for six months in three different places." [48] Two other priests also gave witness to the letter's original receipt on February 4, 1988. They are Father Vinko Orgicevic and Father Luca Susac.

As a pilgrim in Medjugorje, I've seen Vicka speaking publicly several times after September 1988. I neither saw nor heard any evidence to suggest that Vicka has had any reoccurrence of the brain tumor since she was healed of it twenty-four years ago. Granted, Vicka has been asked to accept other illness since then. She's done so humbly, but I've seen no evidence of any brain tumor. If you wish to read further about Medjugorje healing stories, there's also the book written by Larry and Mary Sue Eck called *Medjugorje Miracles of Physical Healings*. The book can be purchased by going to www.amazon.com or to the Eck's website for *Medjugorje Magazine*: www.medjugormag.com Described in their book are the healing stories of Colleen Willard, also Artie Boyle's, Jerry Drumm's, Loretta Young's, and a number of others.

The remainder of this chapter transitions now to exploring other signs and wonders that have been characteristic of the Medjugorje event. There's been a large number of these incidents reported, witnessed by a great number of people. Signs such as these are intended to strengthen the faith of the people affected by them. They've affected my own faith. I'll describe now the specific signs that I saw while walking through the outlying areas of Medjugorje in late October 1990.

The Incident of the Burning Bush

It was a damp, drizzly day, and I was just praying quietly on Podbrdo (Apparition Hill) in Medjugorje. I was near the metal cross anchored by rocks, which then marked the site of the first apparition (pictured below). Today at that same spot, the parish now has a small shrine and white statue of Our Lady under the title "Queen of Peace."

My dad was with me and we had climbed Apparition Hill together. It began to get a little dark, and since it was drizzling, he recommended that we begin the descent to the bottom of the mountain. We began moving and decided to say five decades of the rosary on the walk down. We were about halfway through the rosary when my dad turned around toward me and said, "Go ahead, son."

"What do you mean?" I replied.

He answered (somewhat annoyed), "Finish your half." We had some confusion because I thought that I had just finished saying my half of the Hail Mary (he was saying the first half and I was saying the second).

So I said to him, "I just finished it." Either he didn't hear me or I never did say the second half (I'm not certain, but I thought I did). Regardless, in the confusion of him turning around to say this to me, he slipped on a rock and tripped. As he fell, his hand brushed aside a thorn on a bush, and he started bleeding a little. Getting up, he was looking toward the top of the mountain, far to the right of the cross.

"Turn around and look up there," he said. I turned around and saw—way off in the distance—a very large burning bush. It was completely engulfed in flames! At first, I tried to think of a rational explanation.

"Looks like somebody started a big fire," I said to him. He was thinking much more in terms of a supernatural sign.

"That's impossible," he said, again sounding kind of annoyed at me. "It's been raining for two days. The ground is saturated. Nobody could have started a fire like that." I then started to think it *was* a sign. The ground was, in fact, very wet that day.

Was *the burning bush* a supernatural sign? After much reflection, I've concluded that it was. I base my opinion on the fact that I'm one of many who have seen holy ground in Medjugorje lit up with fire and other unexplainable signs. Unexplainable lights, fires, and signs with the sun had already been reported numerous times in Medjugorje according to Father Rene Laurentin in his book *Is the Virgin Mary Appearing in Medjugorje?* (1984). The witnessing of fire was an issue that had been previously brought to the visionaries' attention: "The visionaries asked the Gospa . . . regarding the fire that hundreds of people saw that burned but did not consume anything (on Mount Krizevac).

'The fire, seen by the faithful,' the Virgin answered in response, 'was of a supernatural character. It is one of the signs, a forerunner of the Great Sign'" (October 28, 1981).[49] Thus, the Virgin confirmed in 1981 this had happened there before and that such a sign had been sent from heaven.

What Is the Great Sign?

The previous quote from Mary refers to the Great Sign. Especially in 1981, the visionaries asked Mary repeatedly about her promise of this great and permanent physical sign to be left on the hill called Podbrdo. Below are comments made by Our Lady about the Great Sign. The first was in response to the visionary Ivan who asked when Our Lady will leave the sign. "The sign will be given at the end of the apparitions"[50] (Virgin Mary, September 4, 1981). Our Lady adds, "Pray especially on Sunday so that the Great Sign, the gift of God, may come"[51] (September 6, 1981). Mary responds to additional questions from the visionaries about the Great Sign, "You are not to ask me any more questions on the subject of the (Great) Sign. Do not be afraid. It will surely appear. I carry out my promises. As far as you are concerned, pray, persevere in prayer"[52] (October 26, 1981). "Be converted, all of you who are still here. The sign will come when you are converted"[53] (September 9, 1981). "It is mine to realize the promise. With regard to the faithful, have them pray and believe firmly"[54] (October 17, 1981).

Small Shrine and Statue on Apparition Hill (Below) Which Now Mark Site of First Apparition in 1981

The Sign of Wayne Weible

The second sign I received personally on the 1990 pilgrimage related to a man I'd never met and who has become one of Medjugorje's most popular writers. He would also lead numerous pilgrim groups to this holy place, and I would join his group three times in the future years. Already an established journalist before hearing of Medjugorje, this former Lutheran converted to Catholicism and became a successful writer on these events after he heard the Virgin Mary speak to him while watching a video about the visions. Soon thereafter, he published his first of several books on the apparitions, *Medjugorje: The Message.* The author's name is Wayne Weible. One of the men in our tour group on the '90 pilgrimage had become familiar with Wayne by this point. He was walking with me and my dad to go over and climb Apparition Hill. This incident happened on the same day as the burning bush, but it took place before we began to descend from the hill and saw the fire.

During the walk over to the hill, the man said something like, "You know something, I really don't believe in all this apparition business. I have a really hard time believing that the Mother of God is appearing here." Wayne Weible would have something to do with changing his disbelief.

My dad said to him, "If you received some kind of a sign, would you believe then?"

"What kind of a sign?" the man inquired.

"What kind of a sign do you want?" my dad replied.

The man said back, "Okay, well . . . (and he thought about it a few moments) . . . If I see Wayne Weible sometime while I'm here on pilgrimage, I'll become a believer."

We acknowledged this man's request to see Wayne as his sign and we kept walking. We began our ascent up Apparition Hill at about three in the afternoon. On the way up the half-hour or so climb, the three of us prayed the rosary. We then came to a location where people gathered around the site of the first apparition.

At this point, my dad said to this man, "Look over to the group of people standing near the cross. Do you see anyone you recognize?"

Both this man and I looked over toward the cross. The man then acknowledged that standing right there with the group of people was the middle-aged Medjugorje author.

"That's Wayne Weible!" he exclaimed. He was partly in a state of bewilderment and partly in a state of excitement. "I can't believe it. That's Wayne Weible!"

I asked my dad and this other man which person Wayne was since I didn't know what Wayne looked like.

"He's right over there," my dad replied (pointing toward him). "He's wearing a dark-colored leather jacket, he's about forty-five, and he's got short black hair." I saw the man who met this description.

I count this incident as a sign because of what it did for this man in his faith walk and how the Virgin brought him together with Wayne. While some may pass it off as a coincidence, consider his witness when we returned back to our hotel. The man had split off from us after he received his sign in order to pray privately on the hill. He arrived back, ironically, at the same time we were entering the front door of the hotel.

He asked us (alluding back to the first sign I saw), "Did you see the size of the fire on the hill?"

"Yes," we both replied.

"That was really something, wasn't it?" I asked.

"I'll say," he replied. "Between that and seeing Wayne today, I believe now! *I believe Our Lady is appearing in Medjugorje!*"

Silver and Gold

The third sign I'll describe wasn't recognized until after I returned home to Boston after the '90 pilgrimage ended. Two women from my hometown of Norwood, Betty and Ann, asked me to take their rosaries to Medjugorje to have them blessed there by a priest. I did so and afterward returned the rosaries to them. They were stunned to see that the metal links on the rosaries had changed colors. I didn't notice it before, but they told me that the links on their beads had been silver before. Now they said they were *gold.* I took a close look, and they sure did look gold to me. This sign is reported often in Medjugorje related to rosary beads. A dozen or so people have witnessed this phenomenon to me concerning the changed color of the metal links on their rosaries. They each reported a change in color from silver to gold. It's probably a way for the Holy Mother to affirm the practice and use of the rosary in our prayer lives.

Don't Try This at Home

I intentionally left the next sign last for this chapter because I don't want to emphasize it too much due to the risk associated with it. My dad and I were standing off to the side of St. James Church at about four in the afternoon. We noticed a number of people looking in the direction of the sun. I thought perhaps that they all saw something in the sky. I looked up but saw nothing unusual. We soon realized that they were all staring directly into the sun for an extended period. We didn't know what they were seeing or why they were doing this, but I thought it was strange for them to keep looking into this strong brightness. My dad also tried looking and then encouraged me to look up at the sun. I said okay, but then I put on my sunglasses. I looked at the sun, and then slowly, I titled the sunglasses down. At first, I felt a strain, but within a few seconds, the strain disappeared while I kept looking. Then the sun's brightness really faded as it became eclipsed by a white circle. The circle looked very much like the Eucharist and eclipsed most of the sun so that I could only see the outer edges of the sun's yellow color. I interpreted this as a sign. I saw this as a sign that Jesus was at the center of these events. I believe this was meant to direct me to receive him more often in Holy Communion. I continued to look at the sun for ten minutes and it was no problem. Nonetheless, I'd strongly recommend that nobody try this at home. I don't want to encourage people to try doing this except, perhaps, if you're in Medjugorje. Even there, if the strain doesn't go away within a few seconds, I wouldn't keep looking because you could cause permanent damage to your retina and eyesight.

God of Wonders

I'll finish this section by mentioning briefly a few other unusual signs in the village. Mary comments in response to questions regarding these other phenomena:

October 22, 1981. They (the visionaries) ask if the whiteness of the cross (on Mount Krizevac) is a supernatural phenomenon.

"Yes, I confirm it," Mary responded.[55] Many saw the cross transform itself into a light and then into a silhouette of Our Lady.

She comments, "All of these signs are designed to strengthen your faith until I leave you the visible and permanent sign." [56]

October 25, 1981. The visionaries asked Our Lady about the great light three girls saw on their way home from Mass. Within the light, they saw fifteen figures.

"It was a supernatural phenomenon," Mary explained. "I was among the saints." [57]

This concludes the discussion about all the signs, wonders, and healings related to Medjugorje. After returning from this pilgrimage, it was only another month or two before I called the local seminary to say that I wanted to apply for admission. I'd been exploring this idea in spiritual direction for about a year. After applying, I had an interview with the seminary rector in January 1991. Apparently, I passed the interview, as well as psychological tests shortly thereafter. The final step of the screening process was an April interview at the seminary with four priests. Within a month after that, I received my acceptance letter, which welcomed me to begin pretheology studies at the diocesan seminary in Massachusetts beginning in the fall. Simultaneously, I completed my goal of doing three years of service in the public accounting profession. It turned out to be three and a half years. Satisfied with that and with the formal acceptance into the seminary, I decided to resign from the accounting job in May. Studies would begin soon enough, so I decided not to stay in public accounting through the summer. I did some volunteering instead for a nonprofit group that promoted the message of Medjugorje. I worked alongside a young man named Joe Medio. I'd never met Joe before, but he told me he was from my hometown of Norwood, Massachusetts. I asked him how he got to volunteering for the nonprofit group. He said he'd read a book about the message of Medjugorje and that it was changing his life. Later, Joe also applied to the seminary I was going to, and he came in to study about a year after me. After completing a year, he transitioned to become a Franciscan novice. To make a long story short, he's now Father Joseph Medio, a Franciscan priest with the order called the Friars of the Primitive Observance. Father Joe's story could be considered yet another sign sent through the work of Our Lady of Medjugorje. Some signs are small signs, some medium, some very big. I'd say Joe's vocation was a rather big one. Mary's words below concern the Great Sign that is to come. We should not overlook the person of Jesus in this discussion. Everything about this subject is meant to strengthen our faith in Christ. He's the one who saves and heals us. I mentioned that I looked up and saw the sun. Perhaps the words on the front cover of a recent *Medjugorje Magazine* would state it better. It reads: "I Saw the Son."

These are Our Lady's words about the Great Sign:

> This sign will be given for the atheists. You faithful already have signs and you have to become the sign for the atheists. You faithful must not wait for the sign before you convert: convert soon. This time is a time of grace for you. You can never thank God enough for this grace. This time is for deepening your faith and for your conversion. When the sign comes, it will be too late for many. [58] (reported words of Our Lady of Medjugorje in the earlier days of the apparitions according to an article by Medjugorje author and source, Wayne Weible)

Chapter 4

Pilgrimage

When I was in my fourth year in the seminary, I returned to Medjugorje in 1995 with two other seminarians, Michael and John. This was the third time I traveled to Medjugorje on pilgrimage. It was August, and it was very hot there, but we didn't seem to care. The absence of air-conditioning in our shared room didn't deter us from having a very positive and uplifting Medjugorje experience. We just happened to pick a pansion without AC, so we kept the windows open and the fan on. Mike and John were terrific pilgrims to go with. They were great company and are very positive and spiritual young men. Mike went on to become a priest in Boston, and John decided that priesthood wasn't for him. He left the seminary, found a young lady, and later decided to get married.

I was ordained a Catholic priest in 1996. I'd been a parish priest just over a year and was stationed at St. Bernard's Parish in West Newton, Massachusetts, when I sensed a call to lead and organize a pilgrimage to Medjugorje with some laypeople. This would turn out to be my fourth pilgrimage, which took place in May 1998. We promoted it within the parish after getting some clearance from our pastor, Father Barry. He wasn't that comfortable with Medjugorje and told me that he'd rather I take people to Fatima or Lourdes. I said that, yes, those trips would be great opportunities too, but I wanted to encourage the people to come to a place where the

Madonna was reported to appear presently. He went along with it, but reluctantly.

Twenty-four people signed up for the May pilgrimage. I was glad the number was neither too big nor too small. I was happy to have joined this group from St. Bernard's and surrounding parishes. One of the people who signed up to join us was my mother, Patricia. My mom had made a trip of her own to Medjugorje in 1989 but wanted to go back. I want to relate a special experience I was fortunate to have had with my mother the night before the pilgrimage ended. The parish hosts Holy Hours of Adoration and Benediction of the Blessed Sacrament on Wednesday and Saturday nights. We were scheduled to leave on a Sunday, so we both decided to go to the adoration service the night before. We didn't plan to stay for the whole hour though, because we needed to finish packing and get ready to depart the next morning. We were forty-five minutes into the service, and it was getting close to 10:00 p.m., but by then, neither of us cared about the time anymore. We were overwhelmed by the strong presence of grace that was coming from the period of adoration. We didn't want to leave. There was a strong peace that we both witnessed to each other after the service ended. The clock went past ten as the Benediction concluded, but again, we didn't care anymore about the practicalities of preparing for departure. The Lord was at center stage, and he had something very special to share with us on that evening. After the service ended and they were closing the church doors, other pilgrims from our group invited us to the popular Colombo's restaurant to get some dessert. I don't recall when the packing actually got done, but I remember very well joining the group and capping the trip off with some ice cream. I'm glad my mom came along for the trip with us. She is a spirit filled and very faithful Catholic and she is a very positive person. She taught me, mostly by example, the meaning of service, generosity, faith, and kindness.

The purpose of this chapter is to take a look at Medjugorje from the experience and vantage point of the pilgrimage. I wrote this chapter while sitting before the spot where the six visionaries say the Mother of God first appeared on Apparition Hill in Medjugorje. Marking that spot, there is a small shrine that has a white statue of Mary with the caption *Ja sam Kraljica Mira* (Croatian for "I am the Queen of Peace"). I've seen a large number of the faithful climb to and from this spot, and my experience is that this is a very holy place. A consistent theme emerged as I kept reading and hearing about the Medjugorje message. We've been reminded through Mary's lengthy visitation and repeated words that this period has been *a time of grace* meant for the *deepening of faith* and for the *conversion of sinners*.

From pilgrimage to pilgrimage, I grew to comprehend that the Medjugorje event and message is directed to everyone. This is because the world has required a major intervention from heaven and one that encourages us in the faith. This is also meant in a special way to persuade those not following God's ways to choose for spiritual conversion and salvation in Jesus Christ. For those who have fallen away or aren't practicing their faith, the Holy Mother's message exhorts such people to awaken spiritually and to begin living by faith. We're reminded that God exists and is calling us out of love to draw closer to him. The miracle at Medjugorje is lengthy because God wants to give all people in the world mercy, time, grace, and a chance to be saved in Christ. God wants each and every person to be saved. He also wants us to discover peace and to be protected from chaos and disorder caused by those powers of the world that have abandoned God to go their own way. This is the perspective I've grown to understand about this phenomenon since the time I first began to travel there. I hope I've begun to establish a good case on the side of the "defense." If you're still questioning it, there's more to consider in the paragraphs to follow.

Consistencies

Four consistencies about Medjugorje speak to its credibility as a place of Marian apparitions and divine intervention.

The first consistency over these years has been the very strong presence of Holy Mass and Eucharist (i.e., Communion). Even if you're not Catholic or don't attend Mass, it may be refreshing to see this many people flocking to church services constantly. There's been a revival and anointing here that keeps people coming in large numbers. Mass is said in various languages throughout the day in St. James Church, the local parish of Medjugorje. Each day, there's a Mass in English, Italian, German, and twice in Croatian. In a nearby chapel called the Adoration Chapel, pilgrim groups also arrange to have Mass said in other languages. Each week, the parish hosts holy hours of Eucharistic adoration, accompanied by spiritual music. These have ordinarily been done every Wednesday and Saturday evenings. The services are well orchestrated and very well coordinated between the various musicians and the worship leader. The church is usually filled to beyond capacity. When the weather is warm enough, the services are done outside behind the main church, where there's much more room for everyone. Adoration gives many the opportunity to enter into a deep spiritual encounter with Christ in the holy sacrament. An additional period of adoration is also offered on Thursday, in thanksgiving, following the evening Mass.

The second consistency I want to emphasize is the constant stream of penitents one sees standing in line for confession in the hours prior to and during evening services. Even as I write this chapter in the colder month of December, I've seen about forty people standing outside to go to confession each weeknight. Even if you're not Catholic or don't believe in confession, is it not good to see many people want to make amends with God for past sins and practice repentance? An extraordinary number of youth have been to confession in Medjugorje and began changing their ways and turning their lives over to Christ. In his book, *The Drama of Medjugorje,* Jesuit author Rev. Richard Foley gives witness to Medjugorje's grace for confession: "Medjugorje has surely brought about much joy before the angels of God over so many sinners receiving the sacrament of penance—and continuing to do so on a regular basis."[59] Father

Foley quotes Father Rene Laurentin on the same subject: "It is that place where more confessions are heard than anywhere in the world, as many as one hundred fifty confessors being kept busy on some days. Moreover, you also find there the highest proportion of 'conversion' confessions—such as bring about a reform of lives sunk in materialism and perversion, the reconciliation of spouses, not to mention other kinds of spiritual fruit."[60] One catalyst for the surge in confessions is the call of Our Lady of Medjugorje to make going to confession a monthly practice. "To quote Mary's words as communicated through her human mouthpiece, Mirjana, 'One must invite people to go to confession each month, especially the first Saturday . . . Monthly confession will be a remedy for the church in the west. One must convey this message to the west (August 6, 1981) . . . I am happy because you have begun to prepare the monthly observance of the sacrament of reconciliation. That will be good for the whole world'" (October 1, 1982).[61]

A third consistency is the holiness and serenity of places like Apparition Hill and Krizevac (or Cross Mountain). I've walked up Apparition Hill and Krizevac numerous times. Apparition Hill is the easier climb and Krizevac the more difficult. When adopting the spirit of prayer (sometimes penance), the climbing seems less of a burden. These are holy places, and one can sense the presence of God there in a special way. When I reach the top of Krizevac or when I reach the Marian statue on Apparition Hill, God seems very close and prayer is easier. Even on the way up, there is grace, but you have to stop now and then to experience it. Because so many others have also given witness to the holiness of places like this in the village, the bishops of the region have identified Medjugorje as "a holy place, a sanctuary, and a place of prayer." [62]

A Picture of the Author on Krizevac (Cross Mountain) in Medjugorje, 2009

The fourth consistency about Medjugorje is the witness and authenticity, in my opinion, of the six visionaries. Each year since 1981, they've continued with their public testimony of the appearances of the Mother of God. In front of their homes, at other public places in Medjugorje, in the United States, Europe, and throughout the world, they've given this testimony to a great many people. In doing so, they've withstood the responsibility and pressures of countless pilgrim visits and questions, as well as the careful scrutiny of Catholic priests and bishops. This isn't to mention media attention, interviews, and numerous rounds of psychological tests. The tests have proven they are normal and not lying (refer to appendix 2). In the earlier days of the apparitions, they even faced harassment from the police and the Communist government. On the fourth day of the visions, June 27, 1981, local Communist authorities took the young people in for questioning to a police station in nearby Citluk. The authorities had them examined by a doctor, with the hope that they could be declared mentally unstable. A Dr. Ante Vujevic, however, had only given Ivan an adequate examination before Vicka was able to pressure the doctor into releasing them. She explained that it was late in the afternoon, and the time for that day's vision was drawing closer. The doctor later said that he could not identify anything wrong with the visionaries. The various psychological tests cited in appendix 2 also provide evidence that the six visionaries are considered stable and psychologically healthy individuals.

What the visionaries experienced that day alone of June 27, 1981, lends greater credibility to their overall witness. After having to transition from police headquarters in neighboring Citluk, the visionaries came to the familiar hill to see some five thousand people gathered to join them for the expected vision. A complex series of affairs ensued that teenagers would have a very hard time concocting on their own. After arriving to climb the hill called Podbrdo, the visionaries lost each other in the crowd and were scattered on the mountain. A bright light flashed, which drew them to a common spot within a very short period of time. Somehow, each made their way through the crowd, seemingly unaffected by the thorn bushes and rocky ground. The Virgin then appeared not once, but six times that evening! I won't describe all the visions, but on two occasions, Our Lady was reported to appear and then disappear because both times someone had stepped on her veil. The visionaries were shocked that the people came up so close behind and in front of them and stepped on the veil, but the crowd was not in control. The visionaries' adult friend and bodyguard, Marinko, cleared space around the children since the crowd was pressing in so much, even infringing on Mary's space while she was appearing. Granted, they could not see Mary, but a number of people did not seem to respect the space around the visionaries. Finally, things settled down and the vision proceeded as it normally had during the previous three days. Jakov put forward a question to the Madonna and asked what was expected from the Franciscans in Medjugorje. The response came: "Have them persevere in the faith and protect the faith of the people."[63] To the people at large, her advice was, "Let those who do not see believe as if they see."[64] Mirjana and Jakov expressed concern because some people were treating them like liars. Our Lady responded, "Do not be afraid of injustices. They have always existed."[65] Ivan was not present for this apparition. He respected the wishes of his mother, who asked him to stay home after his interrogation. She was afraid of the growing attention her son was getting from the police. Ivan felt dejected but was comforted by a private vision of Mary later, one of the six referred to that day. Ivan related that Mary told him to be "at peace" and to "take courage."[66] She then smiled as she bade him farewell. Perhaps because the other five seers needed some reassurance and calming after being in the large crowd, Our Lady appeared to them once again after they had been set apart and were returning home. She simply said, "Farewell, my angels. Go in the peace of God!"[67]

Father Jozo Zovko was the Franciscan pastor of the Medjugorje parish, St. James Church, at this time. He was away during the initial days of the visions, leading a retreat for nuns in Zagreb. He came back on the twenty-seventh to see his village filled with cars, trucks, tractors, donkey carts, and a great many people walking about. He was startled by this and was apparently not yet aware of all that was taking place. He first listened to a tape recording of interviews with the seers conducted earlier by his assistant pastor, Father Zrinko Cuvalo. As soon as he could, he interviewed the seers. At first, he didn't believe them and sternly said to Jakov, "You did not see her!" Little Jakov retorted, "I saw the Madonna! I saw her as if she were in front of me. I saw her as I see you!" he maintained.[68] The young people had the forty-year-old pastor conflicted and second-guessing himself. On one hand, he was a bit skeptical that the Madonna would choose children he considered quite ordinary, and he also discovered some slight differences in the way they reported things. He was impressed though with the consistency by which they described her appearance. They all described her as looking "about twenty years old, indescribably beautiful, with blue eyes, black hair, wearing a white veil and a bluish-grey robe, hovering just above the ground, and with a crown of twelve stars just above her head."[69] With regard to some differences in reporting various encounters with the Virgin, this does not hurt the case of a visionary's credibility: "The greatest mistake . . . is to expect visionaries (if there are more than one) to relate their messages in exactly the same way. Subjectivity and differences in experiencing, receiving, transmitting, and explaining messages are not arguments against authenticity, but speak in its favor. To report a supernatural experience (such as a vision) 'objectively,' every individual must use his or her own expressions, metaphors, and descriptions A good example of this is the four gospels in which the mystery of Christ is presented in different ways" (Fr. Svetozar Kraljevic, OFM, refer to appendix 5).

June 27, 1981, was just one day out of the many days that the visionaries have experienced in their profound and extraordinary roles. This fourth day of the visions gives us a glimpse into what they've endured. It's been a long, consistent, and faithful witness. Their job is often stressful. People have tried to disprove them, and they are constantly asked the same kinds of questions. For them to persevere has required patience and fortitude. To this day, they continue to witness publicly to what they've been saying all along—the Blessed Mother has been appearing to them and giving them many messages. After thirty-one years, we must answer the question, "Have they already passed the test of time?"

Surprises and Signs

If you go to Medjugorje, be prepared for surprises and unexpected ways of getting prayers answered. There are lots of small signs, sometimes a bigger one or a miracle. I've experienced such signs myself, as reported in chapter 3. I've heard others witness to unexplainable incidents so many times that I cannot disbelieve that Jesus and the Blessed Virgin have worked powerfully and generously here. There are too many coincidences to think that heaven is not acting in a favorable way to help the many pilgrims. Mary has a way of working things out or bringing things together in Medjugorje. As people of faith, however, our objective should not be about looking for signs from heaven. Jesus said, "An evil and adulteress generation craves for a sign, and yet no sign will be given to it, but the sign of Jonah the prophet" (Matthew 12:38-40).[70] Our *faith*, not signs, should lead us forward in our journey with God. Faith has to do with what is not seen or proven. Our father in faith, Abraham, had to go completely on faith when God asked him to gather all his belongings and move from the territory of Haran "unto a land that I will show thee" (Genesis 12:1). That was to the land of Canaan. It was there to which Abraham was directed to go and settle with his family. He also had to practice faith when God asked him to sacrifice his only son, Isaac. Abraham passed this test of faith because he was just about to slay Isaac before an angel stopped him (Genesis 22:10-12). Consider this definition of faith in Hebrews: "Now faith is the assurance of things hoped for, the conviction of things not seen" (Hebrews 11:1).[71] What kind of a faith journey does one have if it's dependent on signs? Nonetheless, if we do receive a sign, we should try to interpret its meaning and then move on from that point to a deeper level of faith. It's best that we develop our relationship with God from a *faith* perspective and not be caught up with looking for signs. Holy places like Medjugorje are there to help us in that walk. The many signs given there are God's way of trying to encourage people in their faith. Reported visions, signs, healings, and wonders are common. Signs are given because God understands that some people need signs. God heals us because he loves us and responds to prayers that are said with faith in Jesus Christ. All of these good things are a means to an end. The end is faith and salvation in the person of Christ.

Miracle Continues

In its totality, I believe Medjugorje is a strong sign of God's presence, mercy, and activity for our age. The Virgin has encouraged many to make the pilgrimage to this place. My experience has been that I discovered special graces there, especially the grace to pray more easily and often. Perhaps you, the reader, have not yet traveled to Medjugorje and are considering an experience over there. Maybe you've been there already and want to go back. People who respond to an invitation of the Madonna can somehow find a way to get over there even if finances are tight. If a person is poor and Mary wants them to come over, someone else will often pay for their travel expenses. I've never heard of anyone experiencing injury while traveling to or from Medjugorje. Even during the civil war in that area from 1991-1995, I didn't hear of one Medjugorje pilgrim getting injured. If you want to go, I hope you have the chance to experience it. From Boston, you can get there by first taking about a seven-hour overnight flight to Europe and then a second flight of one or two hours from there into a city in Croatia and then a two-and-a-half-hour bus ride from that city into Medjugorje. The second flight can alternatively land in Sarajevo, Bosnia-Herzegovina, but you will still have about a two-and-a-half-hour bus ride into Medjugorje. For Americans, I recommend to stay overnight at a hotel near the first European airport you land before boarding the next flight into Croatia or Sarajevo. For example, you could stay at a hotel in Frankfurt or Munich, Germany, or in Vienna. I'd save the second flight for the next day. Otherwise, you'll have to do the following after flying all night on the plane across the Atlantic: (1) clear customs at the first airport in the morning, (2) get on the next flight into Croatia or Sarajevo, (3) get your bags in Croatia or Sarajevo, and (4) take the two-and-a-half-hour bus ride into Medjugorje. The travel can all be done in a day without the hotel stop. However, the trip is less difficult if you break it up with the hotel stay in Europe.

According to Medjugorje's official website, www.medjugorje.hr, statistics indicate that the number of Communion hosts distributed from the Medjugorje parish over a twelve month period surpassed .the 2 million figure for the first time in 2011 (2,027,900 hosts). For the ten-year period 2002-2011, an average of 1.4 million hosts were distributed from the Medjugorje parish each year.[72] The total number of concelebrating priests counted at Mass for the same ten-year period was 321,956.[73] In the most recent year, the number of concelebrating priests exceeded 40,000 for the first time (41,094 priests during 2011). In other words, more people and priests are coming to Medjugorje. So do book ahead if you want to assure yourself a room. The busiest months are the May-October pilgrimage season. You can go any time of year, and certainly the crowds are down very much during the winter months. It usually begins to get hot in June. The July and August months are very hot. May, September, October, and November have more comfortable temperatures. The winter is cloudy, cool, and sometimes very rainy. It's not as cold as a Boston winter, and they have historically had little snow there.

> Dear children! Today I invite you to conversion. This is the most important message that I have given you here. Little children, I wish that each of you become a carrier of my messages. I invite you, little children, to live the messages that I have given you over these years. This time is a time of grace. Especially now, when the church also is inviting you to prayer and conversion, I also, little children, invite you to live my messages that I have given you during the time since I've appeared here. Thank you for having responded to my call.[74] ("Monthly Message to the World," February 25, 1996, given through the visionary Marija Pavlović-Lunetti)

Chapter 5

The Message: What Is She Saying?

At the start of the previous chapter, I made no mention of my first four years in the seminary before jumping ahead to describe the joint pilgrimage with fellow seminarians John and Mike during the summer of 1995. I entered the Boston seminary on September 5, 1991 after resigning from my post as a public accountant. On the day I walked through the seminary doors, I remember being at peace. I'd been trying to live out the five messages of Our Lady of Medjugorje as best I could for three years. Those five practices will be explained in the paragraphs to follow. I'd spend the next five years (excepting summers) confronting rigorous academic studies and other tests and requirements for ordination. I received from my seminary education many theological understandings for which I'm grateful to have obtained. The faculty was a devoted and hardworking group of mostly priests, one religious sister, and laypeople. During the five academic years, I took about forty-five classes. They kept us very busy reading. It was a very disciplined and structured formation program focusing on academic, pastoral, human, and spiritual formation. So the faculty invested much effort toward expanding us in these areas. I clearly spent at least half of my time reading books, studying academics, and going to classes. I can't say if the same structure exists today because that formation took place in the 1990s, and so I honestly don't know. Regarding Medjugorje or apparitions in general, the faculty was reserved toward private revelations or apparitions of any kind. On Medjugorje, the message seemed clear, and they didn't have to post it on the wall for me to grasp it. They didn't consider this that important, and they recommended that I focus on what they were trying to teach me. I can't say I ever consented to the belief that the Medjugorje event was insignificant. I wasn't convinced that was the bishop's belief either and I didn't think it was God's. Though I did place a primary focus on my formation and studies, I never reached a point where I thought the Medjugorje event wasn't that important. I respectfully dissented from their approach on that matter and expressed this to them just before they voted on whether to advance me to the fifth and final year of formation. It was a very close vote, I recall. Five were in favor, three were opposed, two abstained, and one was absent. A seminarian needed majority for that vote, and they considered the five votes a majority under those circumstances. One less vote and I would have been held back. Four to four would not have cut it because the seminarian had to have at least one vote greater than a tie vote. I passed the many tests and evaluations and, following the fifth year of formation, was ordained a priest by the bishop of my diocese on May 25, 1996. The first two years of the seminary formation were positive experiences in general and moved along smoothly. I found the last three years to be painfully difficult for many reasons that are too complex to relate in this chapter or book. These reasons would be very distracting from the message of Medjugorje, which this chapter concerns.

If you were to vote as to whether Medjugorje is important, how would you decide? I think Medjugorje embodies something important not just for the church but for the whole world. I would now like to transition to looking at the words that the Holy Mother is reported to convey. Part of her message is a call to be her human messengers to others about what she's saying. I perceived her commissioning while I was in the seminary and was trying to comply with what I thought she was asking me to do.

The next few chapters communicate what specific messages the Mother of God has reportedly been giving. The present chapter is at the center of what the message of Medjugorje is all about. You'll find specific quotes from other sources as to how the Virgin spoke of these practices. The next chapter will develop these themes more practically as they relate to "spiritual warfare." Chapter 5 is more thematic and explanatory in nature, focusing on the five central recommendations. Chapter 6 deals with the nuts and bolts of what to do in specifically living out the five basic themes. For example, chapter 5 names prayer as one of the five messages and chapter 6 identifies, as one means of prayer, to read the Bible.

From the Beginning

The Virgin Mother explained and summarized during her first week of appearances in June 1981 why she was here and what message it was that she wanted to convey to the people in Medjugorje, to the Balkans, and to the rest of us throughout the modern world. It's important to take a close look at what she said during these first seven days. As I've reflected on those messages, it's clear she was calling everyone to repentance and conversion, as well as to discover peace within and among ourselves and with God. This must be accomplished with a firm faith, reconciliation with God, and through forgiveness of one another.

On the third day of the apparitions, June 26, 1981, Mary said to the six visionaries, "I have come because there are many true believers here. I wish to be with you to convert and to reconcile the whole world" (June 26, 1981).[75]

She also said on June 26, 1981, "Peace, peace, peace! Be reconciled. Only peace. Make your peace with God and among yourselves. For that, it is necessary to believe, to pray, to fast, and to go to confession."[76]

These early messages of June 26, 1981, encapsulate the essence of Mary's whole future message, repeated many times. The message is: (1) peace, (2) faith, (3) conversion, (4) prayer, and (5) fasting (or penance). If you want the first (peace), it's necessary to have firm faith in God, repent/convert (turn away from sin), pray often, and fast / do penance.

Forgiveness and Reconciliation

We must become reconciled with God and try to be reconciled with one another and within ourselves. Forgiveness and reconciliation are elements of conversion. We'll have little peace as long as we're at odds with God or have ill will toward a human person. At the same time, we can't force people to reconcile with us. Sometimes, the best we can do is to simply forgive them. We may also need to forgive ourselves, to "forgive" God (if you're angry at God), to forgive priests, the church, or to forgive our neighbor. This is an essential part of the peace plan Mary has spelled out.

In reconciling with another, it can be both very simple yet very hard. It's hard because it may require that we renounce pride. Sometimes we must go and say the difficult words "I'm sorry. I didn't mean to upset you. Please forgive me." If they have something *against you*, you may need to say, "What's wrong? Are you mad at me for something?" If we're angry with someone but they don't know that, we may need to say, "I'm upset with you," or just point out why their behavior is bothering us. If you're waiting for the other person to come to you or apologize to you, don't hold your breath. Many people seem to have a hard time doing this. That's been my experience. Only on rare occasions have I had a person come to me after doing something wrong and say, "I'm sorry. I messed up." I've had to say numerous times to people, "Sorry about that" or "I apologize." Sometimes, I would have preferred getting a tooth pulled. If I did not do this though, the silence could continue for months because the other one was not able to bridge the gap or communicate. Sometimes we must be the one. We must be the Christian. Mary said, "Be reconciled," not "Dear children, be reconciled after others apologize to you." If you can't apologize (or don't feel you should have to), then can you be the one who will at least put an end to the silence that exists between the two of you? Can you communicate anger or hurt? Even if you can't, there's always ways to talk that puts an end to standoffs. I've had rifts with people that were even broken by talking about the weather, a news story, or something about a sports team. Do whatever you have to do, but in the end "be reconciled" so you can have your peace. Start with prayer and ask what you should do.

The Necessity of Faith

It's not possible to make progress in any of these spiritual areas without faith. Faith is foundational. It's the cornerstone on which the other graces are built. During the first week of the visions, Mary stressed repeatedly the necessity of *faith*. Consider these words she communicated to the six seers the first week:

"Blessed are those who have not seen and who believe" (June 26, 1981)[77]

(This was the Virgin's response to the visionaries when they requested a sign for others, to prove that the apparition was really the Gospa.)

Jakov wanted to know what the Virgin expected of the Franciscans in Medjugorje:

"Have them persevere in the faith and protect the faith of the people" [78] (June 27, 1981).

The visionaries wanted to know what the Gospa wishes:

"That people believe and persevere in the faith" (June 28, 1981).[79]

Vicka asked her, "What do you expect from the priests?"

"That they remain strong in the faith and that they help you" (June 28, 1981).[80]

Three times Vicka asked, "Dear Gospa, what do you expect of these people?"

"That those who do not see believe as those who do see" (June 28, 1981).[81]

They questioned Our Lady about her expectations about those who came despite the heat and the brambles:

"There is only one God, one faith. Let the people believe firmly and do not fear anything" (June 29, 1981). [82]

The visionaries asked her, "What do you expect of us?"

"That you have a solid faith and that you maintain confidence" (June 29, 1981). [83]

Again and again, Mary pleads for strong and firm faith. She asks those who do not see to believe as if they do see. These are the essential basics of a simple yet reasonable faith. God asks us to believe. It's much better to believe without requiring God to prove his existence or the Virgin's appearances. Yet, God will ultimately give proof to those who require it. However, the blessing is on those who believe without seeing (John 20:29). This is the essence of faith, for "faith is the assurance of things hoped for, the conviction of things not seen" (Hebrews 11:1, NASB).

Summarizing the Messages

I will now take the five central messages and have them explained in more depth. In this regard, I will incorporate the words and summaries of a Franciscan priest who relates each of the messages to sacred scripture. His name and credentials are indicated below. I have presented the grammar as it came from my source so as to not take away anything that was intended by the writer.

Father Ljudevit Rupčić, Professor of theology and translator of sacred scripture into the Croatian language [84]

PEACE

Already on the third day, Our Lady stressed peace as the first of her messages: "Peace, peace, peace and only peace!" after which she said twice, "Peace must reign between God and man and between people." Considering that Maria could see a cross, when Our Lady gave this message, the obvious conclusion is that this peace comes from God.

God, who through Our Lady in Christ became our peace, (Ephesians 2:14) "For He is the peace between us." This peace, "the world cannot give" (John 14:27), and that's why Christ commanded His apostles to bring it to the world (Matthew 10:11) so that all men could become "sons of peace" (Luke 10:6).

That's why Our Lady as "Queen of Apostles" in Medjugorje specifically refers to herself as "Queen of Peace." Who better than she can more successfully convince today's world, which is faced with the threat of destruction, how great and how necessary peace is.

FAITH

The second of Our Lady's messages is faith. Already on the fourth, fifth, and sixth day of apparitions, Our Lady exhorted those present to have strong faith. Understandably, she repeated this message many times. Without faith we cannot arrive at peace! Not only this but faith is itself an answer to God's Word, which he not only proclaims but actually gives to us. When we believe, we accept God's Word, which in Christ became "our peace" (Ephesians 2:14). Accepting it, the individual becomes a new creature, with a new life of Christ within, and a share in God's nature (1 Peter 1:4, Ephesians 2:18). In this way the individual ensures peace with God and with others.

Once again there is no one who can better understand the necessity and efficaciousness of faith than Our Lady. That's why she stressed it on every occasion and charged the visionaries to bring the light of faith to others. Our Lady presented faith as an answer to everything, no matter whatever people were looking for. She presented it as the prerequisite of all prayer, desires, and demands, relating it to health, wholeness, and to all other human necessities.

CONVERSION

Conversion was another one of Our Lady's frequent messages. This presupposes that she noticed either a weakness or a complete lack of faith in humanity today. And without conversion it is impossible to achieve peace. True conversion means the purifying or cleansing of the heart (Jeremiah 4:14), because a corrupt or "deteriorated" heart is the basis of bad relations, which in turn brings social disorder, unjust laws, base constitutions, etc. Without a radical change of heart, without the conversion of the heart, there is no peace. For this reason, Our Lady continually suggests frequent confession. The request is directed to all without differentiation because, "not one of us is just . . . all have wandered, not one does right" (Romans 3:11-12).

PRAYER

Almost daily, from the fifth day of apparitions onwards, Our Lady recommends prayer. She requests everyone to "pray without ceasing" just as Christ himself taught (Mark 9:29, Matthew 9:38, Luke 11:5-13). Prayer therefore stimulates and strengthens our faith, without which our relationship with God is disordered, as is our relationship with each other. Prayer also reminds us of how close God is to us even in our daily lives: in prayer we acknowledge Him, we give Him thanks for His gifts to us, and we are filled with a hopeful expectancy of that which we need, but particularly our redemption. Prayer solidifies the equilibrium of the individual and aids us in our "ordered relationship with God," without which it is impossible to maintain peace either with God or with our neighbour.

The Word of the Lord acquainted itself with all humanity and awaits humanity's response. It is precisely this that gives prayer its "justification." Our response should be "spoken faith" or "prayer." In prayer, faith animates, renews, strengthens, and sustains itself. In addition to this, man's prayer really bears witness to the Lord Jesus and to the existence of God, thus provoking a response of faith in others.

FASTING

Already on the sixth day of the apparitions, Our Lady often recommended fasting because it aids faith. That is, the practice of fasting aids and ensures control over oneself. Only the person who can dominate himself is truly free and is capable of abandoning himself to God and to his neighbour, as faith demands. Fasting guarantees him that his abandonment to faith is secure and sincere. It helps him to free himself from every slavery, but especially to the slavery to sin. Whoever is not in the possession of oneself is in some way enslaved. Therefore, fasting helps the individual to restrain himself from disordered pleasure seeking, which in turn leads him to a futile and useless existence often wasteful of the very goods that are necessary to others just for basic survival.

With fasting we also retrieve the gift, which creates within us a realistic love for the poor and the destitute, which up to a certain point eases the difference between rich and poor. It therefore heals the wants of the poor and also heals the excesses and overindulgence of others. And in its own way, it gives a dimension of peace that today, in a special way, is threatened by the difference in the lifestyles of the rich and the poor (e.g., North and South).

To sum this up, we can say that Our Lady's messages underline that peace is the greatest good, and that faith, conversion, prayer, and fasting are the means by which we can attain it. This concludes Father Rupčić summary of *the message*. [85]

> Dear children, today I am grateful to you for your presence in this place, where I am giving you special graces. I call each one of you to begin to live as of today that life which God wishes of you and to begin to perform good works of love and mercy. I do not want you, dear children, to live the message and be committing sin which is displeasing to me. Therefore, dear children, I want each of you to live a new life without the * murder of all that God produces in you and is giving you. I give you my Special Blessing and I am remaining with you on your way of conversion. Thank you for having responded to my call. [86] (Our Lady of Medjugorje, "Monthly Message to the World," February 25, 1987)

*("Murder" rather than "destroy" was chosen for the translation of the Croatian word "abidance," because Our Lady used a very strong word meaning *to kill something living.* An automobile as well as a human being can be destroyed. The purest translation is "murder.")[87]

Chapter 6

Spiritual Warfare

Spiritual warfare concerns the challenge each one of us faces in relating to God and one another and persevering in the good, despite the opposition and work of the forces of darkness against and among us. In giving these recommendations, the Virgin Mary wants our happiness. She's not out to place impossible demands on us. She would like us to become less burdened, happy, and at peace. She does not pretend that this is an easy road that is without some sufferings along the way, but her path leads one on the road to a happy destiny. "I want each one of you to be happy here on earth and to be with me in heaven." [88]

Let's get right to the point and identify our spiritual adversary and what I mean by the forces of darkness. Mary acknowledges the work of the devil many times at Medjugorje. She wants us to be aware that he is subtly and invisibly at work in the world with his legions of fallen angels. Consider these words Mary gave to the visionaries to make us aware of the opposition:

"You are ready to commit sin and to put yourselves in the hands of Satan without reflecting" (May 25, 1987). [89]

"Ask everyone to pray the rosary. With it in hand, you will overcome all the troubles which Satan is trying to inflict on the Catholic Church. Let all priests pray the rosary" (June 25, 1985). [90]

"I invite you to place more blessed objects in your homes and to keep some blessed objects on your person. Thus, Satan will attack you less because you will have armor against him" (July 18, 1985). [91]

Father Richard Foley, SJ, relates in *The Drama of Medjugorje*, "The main false fires kindled on the coast of conscience by devils take the form of temptation, which is their stock and trade. The majority of theologians follow St. Thomas (Aquinas) in holding that devils cannot directly read our thoughts or violate our free-will, since they are spiritual functions over which God alone has sovereignty. But they are able to tamper with our imagination, stirring phantasms liable to stimulate sinful thoughts and desires; also they are capable of exciting and disturbing our bodily instincts, including the sexual and the aggressive." [92]

As I consider this reflection of Father Foley's, I am reminded of the modern day's greatest and most common tool of the devil to damage and destroy the children of God: the Internet. The demons are trying to drag down God's people, especially the young, by the many snares and temptations that lay therein! All people who are vulnerable must establish safeguards to protect against the many forms of pornography and other temptations on the Internet. Falling prey to this temptation has already damaged significantly, even destroyed, many lives. Though much good is also on the Internet, Satan has a stronghold there. As long as that stronghold remains established, all must *be on guard*, for a person's thoughts and soul can easily be seduced and harmed. Then one is dragged down and badly damaged.

The following passage from *Words from Heaven* illustrates how the visionary Mirjana was permitted a serious attack from the devil in 1982. The message also sheds light in explaining many of the church's grave struggles throughout the twentieth century and until recently.

She spoke of an apparition in which Satan appeared to her. Satan asked Mirjana to renounce the Madonna and follow him. That way, she could be happy in love and in life. He said that following the Virgin, on the contrary, would only lead to suffering. Mirjana rejected him, and immediately, the Virgin gave her the following message, in substance, "Excuse me for this, but you must realize that Satan exists. One day he appeared before the throne of God and asked permission to submit the Church to a period of trial. God gave him permission to try the Church for one century. 'This century' (message came in 1982) is under the power of the devil, but when the secrets confided to you come to pass, his power will be destroyed. Even now he is beginning to lose his power and has become aggressive. He is destroying marriages, creating division among priests and is responsible for obsessions and murder. You must protect yourselves against these things through fasting and prayer, especially community prayer. Carry blessed objects with you. Put them in your house and restore the use of holy water" (Our Lady of Medjugorje to the visionary Mirjana Dragićević-Soldo, December 25, 1982).[93]

The Weapons

We are not without the means to successfully repel and fight back against all attacks and temptations of the devil. There are spiritual weapons, some of which have already been described in this chapter. Of these, some have been referred to as *"the five weapons"* by Father Jozo Zovko, a Franciscan priest who was pastor of the Medjugorje parish, St. James, when the apparitions began in 1981. Symbolically, he also refers to these weapons as our fives "stones" with which to fight our "Goliath," the devil. The five weapons most accurately fall under the categories of "prayer" and "penance" (from the summary in chapter 5).

Three weapons using prayer:

1. *The Rosary* (recommended daily)—instruction provided in appendix 4. "If you pray, Satan cannot injure you, not even a little, because you are God's children and He is watching over you. Pray, and let the rosary always be in your hands as a sign to Satan that you belong to me" (February 25, 1988). [94]

2. *Mass* (recommended as often as possible but a weekly church service at a minimum). "Mass is the greatest prayer of God. You will never be able to understand its greatness. That is why you must be perfect and humble at Mass, and you should prepare yourselves for it (1983) . . . . You do not celebrate the Eucharist as you should. If you would know what grace and gift you receive, you would prepare yourselves for it each day for an hour at least." [95]

3. *Bible reading* (recommended daily). "You have forgotten the Bible . . . Dear children, today I call you to read the Bible every day in your homes and let it be in a visible place so as always to encourage you to read it and to pray" (October 18, 1984).[96]

Plus two weapons that fall into the category of penance:

1. *Fasting* (recommended Wednesdays and Fridays only). "Fast strictly on Wednesdays and Fridays" (August 14, 1984).[97] The *best* fast identified by Our Lady at Medjugorje is a fast on bread and water. "The best fast is on bread and water. Through fasting and prayer one can stop wars; one can suspend the laws of nature. Works of charity cannot replace fasting . . . everyone except the sick has to fast" (July 21, 1982).[98] Other messages indicate an allowance for variations on the fast based on capacity and personal circumstances. One could also choose to fast from cigarettes, television,

alcohol, or other pleasures: "If you are experiencing difficulties or if you need something, come to me. If you do not have the strength to fast on bread and water, you can give up a number of things. It would be a good thing to give up television, because after seeing some programs, you are distracted and unable to pray. You can give up alcohol, cigarettes, and other pleasures. You yourselves know what you have to do" (December 8, 1981).[99]

If you have a spiritual advisor/director, it would be better to make decisions regarding how to fast or do penance with that director. It is important to pray about how one should respond to this message. The sick are not asked to fast. They have their penance. However, they could try a modified fast if they wanted to and believed they had the strength. I've had a tough time giving up my coffee in recent years. To be quite honest, I've not given it up that much. I used to be able to give it up more easily, but now it is not easy at all. I'd much rather give up chocolate cake than coffee. I think it's better if a person can go without caffeine on fast days. At the same time, if a fast brings on so much suffering that you're miserable and you can't function at all, taking a coffee at the start of the day or the middle should not negate the good that comes from this discipline. Mirjana said Americans often ask her if coffee is okay with the Blessed Mother on the fast days. Mirjana lightly replies: "Sure, as long as you drink it before the Blessed Mother gets up." The goal is to become closer to God, to purify ourselves, and to better control our desires. Good prayer helps one to fast better, and the fast generally moves along with less discomfort if you can set aside time to pray.

2. *Confession.* "Monthly confession will be a remedy for the Church in the West. One must convey this message to the West . . . Do not go to confession through habit, to remain the same after it. No, it is not good. Confession should give

an impulse to your faith. It should stimulate you and bring you closer to Jesus. If confession does not mean anything for you, really, you will be converted with great difficulty." [100] Simply put, the recommendation is to try to go to confession once a month. (Faith traditions other than Catholic who do not have sacramental confession with a priest have recourse to their own ways of treating sin and addressing the need for repentance and confession to trusted others within the community of faith and of believers). I say this ecumenical part on my own and not as a message of Our Lady. It may be close to what Our Lady would recommend from someone who is not Catholic. "Pray, pray! It is necessary to believe firmly, to go to confession regularly and likewise, to receive Holy Communion" (February 10, 1982). [101]

There you have it. This is quite an arsenal. These are the means that are advised and recommended. It is not easy to do all these practices consistently. Is it possible? Yes, with the help of God. We are not expected to do this perfectly, and we will not. To quote a former parish priest of mine, Father Tom DiLorenzo (who spoke more generally in saying this motto), "Do the best you can." That's all God can ask or expect from any one of us. We're not asked the impossible. We are asked, however, to try. So I would recommend one experiment with these means, which are time-honored ways that the saints themselves used in staying in God's good way. Judge for yourself whether doing these things helps increase or regain your peace against any power that would try to thwart its growth within you. The spiritually mature and advancing will be encouraged or even expected by God to use the means that are available to draw close to him and the Virgin. Beginners won't be expected as much, but are reportedly invited by Mary to put her messages into practice. Those that do so will much more easily make advances in the spiritual life, repel the devil, and drive him far away. Those who do not accept or choose to employ that which the Virgin recommends will miss opportunities for greater conversion or peace that may otherwise be found. People need not be in so much turmoil or constant tension since we have the means available to rediscover, find, or keep the peace and order of God in our lives, souls, families, church communities, and workplaces.

Deliverance

A special form of prayer is called *deliverance*. A prayer of deliverance is required when an evil spirit has entered a person. Do I mean that evil spirits can take up real estate within us? Well, yes, I do believe that, if we let them. Usually, such person has opened themselves up to such manifestation by exposing themselves to demonic activity. This can occur by involving oneself with the occult, witchcraft, tarot cards, Ouija boards, levitation, hardcore pornography, the use/purchase/sale of illegal drugs, and other practices in which demons are especially active.

When a person has become infested with a demonic presence, it is essential for him or another person of faith to take authority over that demon and expel it in the name of the Lord Jesus Christ. Any Christian has the authority to say such prayers, but it is very important to know what you are doing and to understand your authority. We have this authority from Christ, who instructed his disciples to cast out demons in his name. Since such authority has been given to us, this means the demons are subject to our authority. So if we tell them to leave by invoking our faith in the name of Jesus, they must comply. However, if the prayers are not said with authority and faith in the Lord Jesus, the demons may not leave. They may stick around until they see we are praying from a place of confidence and faith. The following passage from the Gospel of Luke begins with a report of disciples casting out demons successfully, followed by Jesus's confirmation that this is the authority that has been granted.

> The seventy-two (disciples) returned in jubilation saying,
> 'Master even the demons are subject to us in your name.'

> He (Jesus) said in reply, 'I watched Satan fall from the sky like lightning. See what I have done: I have given you power to tread on snakes and scorpions and all the forces of the enemy, and nothing shall ever injure you. Nevertheless, do not rejoice so much in the fact that the devils are subject to you as that your names are inscribed in Heaven. (Luke 10:17-20)

Would the authority that Christ granted the seventy-two be any less for us today who also believe in Christ? Surely, when a good number of people seem affected by demons just as much today as then, Jesus would want the disciples of today to have the same power. Thus, the Christian should believe he has the power to cast out demons. The Catholic Church and other Christian denominations teach and believe this to be the case, but the church advises caution and prudence in these matters. An example of a prayer of deliverance is as follows:

> Spirits of pornography, lust, and all pornographic spirits from the Internet, I command you in the name of the Lord Jesus Christ to leave. Go immediately, directly, and quietly to the foot of the Cross and remain there until Jesus or his appointed agent sentences you justly. Do no harm to me or anyone else on your way and don't ever return. (It may be necessary to say this repeatedly until the person saying the prayers develops enough confidence and authority to effectively cast out the demons. It is also very good to sprinkle holy water on the person affected and area around him or her).

A person may attempt to practice deliverance on oneself or on others. This is not an exorcism in the formal sense of the word but is still the casting out of an evil presence. It is better to consult with a priest, minister, or another person knowledgeable of the spiritual life before saying such prayers. There can be some danger to involving oneself in this activity. For example, if you are trying to cast out a bad spirit in another person, the spirits may retaliate against the one praying and enter him/her. Before doing this, invoke the Protection Prayer typed just below:

> In the name of Jesus Christ and by the power of his cross and blood, we bind up the power of any evil spirits and command them not to block our prayers. We bind up the powers of the earth, air, fire, water, the netherworld and the satanic forces of nature.
>
> We break any curses, hexes, or spells sent against us and declare them null and void. We break the assignments of any spirits sent against us and send them to Jesus to deal with them as he will. Lord, we ask you to bless our enemies by sending your Holy Spirit to lead them to repentance and conversion.
>
> Furthermore, we bind all interaction and communication in the world of evil spirits as it affects us and our ministry.
>
> We ask for the protection of the shed blood of Jesus Christ over _____ (mention specific names).
>
> Thank you, Lord, for your protection and send your angels, especially St. Michael the Archangel, to help us in the battle. We ask you to guide us in our prayers. Share with us your Spirit's power and compassion. Amen. (source: Christian Healing Ministries, Jacksonville, FL)

The Protection Prayer can be said for oneself and one's family every day, even if the person praying is not specifically doing deliverance on someone at the moment. Also very useful is the prayer to St. Michael the Archangel (typed below). If available, one should apply blessed oil and/or holy water on himself and on the person prayed for. If none are available, the Protection Prayer should be said at a minimum. These measures protect a person from a retaliatory incursion of the demonic while a person is attempting deliverance on another. We upset evil spirits when we say such prayers. It's always possible to be protected from such harm if the right means are employed. For further reading on this subject, try to get the book called *Deliverance from Evil Spirits* by Francis MacNutt. Francis runs Christian Healing Ministries in Jacksonville, Florida.

Deliverance is to be distinguished from an *exorcism*. An exorcism is a formalized rite of the Catholic Church for a person who is possessed by the demonic. I'm not going to get into explaining how a possessed person's condition is more severe, but it is significantly more severe than a person who simply has demons. An exorcism can only be administered by a priest. Further, the priest must be designated by his bishop to perform exorcisms. It cannot be any priest. In recent years, most Catholic dioceses have had an official exorcist, delegated by the bishop for such a need. In fact, I learned recently that the Vatican has ruled that every Catholic diocese must have an official exorcist.

Prayer to St. Michael the Archangel and to one's Guardian Angel

The prayer to St. Michael is a powerful prayer that can help anyone who has been or is being attacked by demons. It is a prayer that has not only been approved by the Catholic Church but it also used to be recited after Mass. I strongly recommend that we renew this practice. Pope John Paul II asked everyone not to forget it and to recite it to obtain help against the forces of darkness. The best way to assure we do this is by saying it together at the conclusion of Sunday services. The prayer is as follows:

Saint Michael the Archangel, defend us in battle. Be our protection against the wickedness and snares of the devil. May God rebuke him, we humbly pray; and do Thou, O Prince of the Heavenly Host—by the Divine Power of God—cast into hell, satan and all the evil spirits, who roam throughout the world seeking the ruin of souls (www.ccel.org/node/4502).

Each person is also given a guardian angel by God. This is a good prayer to your guardian angel. Try to say it often:

Angel of God, my Guardian dear, to whom God's love commits me here, ever this day (or night) be at my side, to light and guard, to rule and guide.

Living the Messages: Qualification and Clarification

You have been challenged in these last two chapters (5 and 6) to adopt and put into practice a series of spiritual activities, which, in their totality, may at first seem overwhelming. It is not the Mother of God's intention to ask more than we can reasonably handle. For these times in which we are living, however, she is recommending a spiritual program that is very ascetical. In other words, she reportedly is calling us through these practices to enter into deep spiritual union with God. The ways she advocates to achieve that will be more than most are accustomed to living out or practicing. Even a monk could feel stretched by her recommendations. Nonetheless, it's indicated that she invites *everyone* to live out her message. That does not mean that she expects each person to be able to respond in the same measure. Her general invitation invites each person to consider factors such as one's capacity and health. She called first the visionaries and then the people of St. James Parish in Medjugorje to respond. Clearly, her messages then went on to invite all who became pilgrims in Medjugorje. Especially since 1987, she began speaking *to the whole world* through the visionary Marija. This message to the world, given on the twenty-fifth of every month, is translated from Croatian into English and many other languages. These messages are published on the website www. medjugorje.hr and numerous other websites dedicated to spreading these messages.

As you've read, her recommendations include a significant emphasis on spending much time in prayer, as well as engaging in acts of voluntary penance, including fasting. I would not describe these as an end, but a stronger means by which to achieve the end that we all seek—knowing God better and trusting him more, stronger faith, happiness, healing, love, peace, salvation, and ultimately heaven. Those are the ends and those are the goals for most people of faith. Mary's goals are no different. By her words, she advises traditional ascetic means by which to strengthen our faith. Faith is central to the message and is the doorway to so many of our goals. It's faith in the person of Jesus that is identified by Our Lady of Medjugorje as the means by which people are healed and saved. Of course, this is consistent with the Bible. Her hope is that we strengthen that faith in Jesus by which we achieve freedom from so many human ills. Also by such faith, we're enabled to discover the peace of God for which Jesus died on the cross.

The Mother of God wants none of her messages watered down. She asks people like me to convey them just as she said them. In her words, "You need the spirit of truth to be able to convey the messages just the way they are, neither adding anything to them, nor taking anything whatsoever away from them, but just the way I said them."[102] In some ways, I find that difficult. I would like to make the more difficult parts easier. Since I've been directed otherwise, I've done the best I could not to do that. I'm a priest though, so I address church teaching in the section below, as it pertains to certain messages and private revelations like Medjugorje. I have to trust that Our Lady would only respect that.

Toward a Free Response

We should respond freely in our application of those messages that the Virgin Mary reportedly communicates at Medjugorje. Some of what is asked may seem (or is) more than what the church ordinarily asks from us. It's my opinion that a person cannot be considered in sin if they don't do everything that is advocated (especially in terms of the more challenging practices related to fasting). I base this on what the Catholic Church has taught me. The church does not oblige the faithful to believe in the specific content of messages coming from apparitions, even if they are later approved. To understand this better, I recommend reading the article from *Glas Koncila,* dated May 5, 1991, in appendix 3. The article explains how the Catholic Church treats public revelations differently from private revelations. Theology classifies apparitions into the category of private revelations. The church only obliges us to adhere to that which has been revealed through public revelation as is found in the Bible. Nonetheless, to the extent that the message of a private revelation corresponds with public revelation, we are obliged to follow it. For example, Christ revealed that we should pray (Matthew 6:5-13). This is a public revelation to which the church obliges belief and practice. Though the church does not oblige belief in private revelations, if the message of such private revelation is also to pray, it is obligatory, but based on the scriptures.

Our Lady of Medjugorje recommends fasting on bread and water strictly on Wednesdays and Fridays. At the same time, the only days of the year when the Catholic Church obliges us to fasting are Ash Wednesday and Good Friday. Canon law recognizes all Fridays of the church calendar as more penitential in nature (with exceptions during the Easter and Christmas seasons, plus feast days that fall on a Friday). However, the church does not oblige us to fast on all those Fridays throughout the year. They encourage more penance and do not discourage fasting, but they do not oblige us to fasting. What Our Lady has asked through the seers, then, may seem radically more than what the church presently asks. It's not a completely new idea since the early church also recognized Wednesdays and Fridays as days of penance and fasting. I learned this in the seminary when reading *The Didache.* Prayer and experience will shed more light for each person on what they should do and what they can do. In my opinion, we need to fast much more than just on Ash Wednesday and Good Friday. That's not nearly enough for the times in which we live.

> You know that I promised you an oasis of peace. But you don't realize that beside an oasis stands the desert where Satan lurks . . . Dear children, only by prayer can you overcome every influence of Satan. (Our Lady of Medjugorje, August 7, 1986) [103]

Chapter 7

The Problem of Materialism

In my early twenties, I was reading the life story of oil tycoon J. Paul Getty as chronicled in *The Great Getty* by Robert Lenzner. I was also reading Donald Trump's *The Art of the Deal.* Ironically, I recall reading these books while on a 1987 trip to Fatima, to which my dad asked me and my sister to accompany him. In between rosary processions at the popular Marian shrine, I was reading about how to become rich.

Early in life, I had begun to develop attachment to money and material things. I was affected by the influence of US culture, media, and attitudes of certain peers wanting to make lots of money. As a college student and later a young professional, I was affected by the Wall Street mentality of the 1980s. I was a business major in college, so I learned how to increase the bottom line, whether for an individual or a corporation. I bought into the world's beliefs that happiness necessitated money and having lots of it. Coming out of college, my intention was to become at least comfortable. If I became rich, that would have been just fine with me.

A Changed Outlook

In Fatima, I apparently had a split devotion. In between times of reciting Hail Marys while riding on a pilgrimage bus with an elder

89

crowd through Portugal, I was sneaking in my next chapter on Getty or Trump. A year or two later though, I began reading *Is the Virgin Mary Appearing at Medjugorje?* by Father Rene Laurentin. I developed a change in perspective after the '88 pilgrimage to Medjugorje, reducing my interest in material wealth. I was taken aback by these words the Virgin Mary had to say: "The West has made civilization progress, but without God, as if they were their own creators" (Our Lady of Medjugorje, October, 1981).[104] The Holy Father gave a remarkably similar assessment during a 2010 speech. On October 11, 2010, Pope Benedict XVI said, "that with tremendous scientific, social, and cultural progress," (Europe and the West, nevertheless) "had grown to believe that they can exist without God." .... "They soon realized the interior desert that is born when man—thinking himself the architect of his own nature and destiny—finds himself lacking that which is fundamental to everything" (ref. note 104).

I didn't like the pop musician Madonna assuming a title of the Virgin Mary. But she was on target when, in her 80s hit song, she sang the words, "We live in a material world and I am a material girl." As my former parish priest Father Tom DiLorenzo described it, we've become the "Kingdom of Thingdom." Put even more plainly, he said, "We've got too much stuff."

Why Is Materialism a Serious Problem?

Materialism gets in the way of our relationship with God. This is why Mary has addressed the problem at Medjugorje. The heart of a materialistic person is concerned more with money and things than with God. At its worst, materialism can destroy our relationship with God. That is because if God is shut out over the long term because money or things are prioritized, people ultimately communicate rejection toward God. Slowly but cleverly, the spirit of materialism draws people gradually away from God to the point where God is, for all intents and purposes, implicitly rejected by default. This is why Pope John Paul II preached against a "practical atheism" in the modern culture. Practical atheism exists when, even though a person doesn't profess to be an atheist explicitly, their atheism is reflected and implied by the way they live. When money and things are the love of one's life and there is no prayer or devotion to God, one lives like a practical atheist.

Please God, we are not living practical atheism. Hopefully, we love God above all things and don't have a problem with materialism. Nonetheless, it is hard not to be distracted frequently by material needs and things in Western culture, especially. Many people face much financial pressure, so they are often preoccupied by what they need or want but do not yet possess. They may be spending much energy and attention each week on simply making ends meet or maybe saving money for the kids' college. They may be preoccupied with the price of gas or the loss in value of their stocks and investments. On the flip side is the problem, if you will, of the rich. Some wealthy have so much that possessions often distract them from the spiritual life. Because they're so secure in what they own, this can often detract from being truly secure in God. Be one rich or poor, there are many good people in these categories who genuinely love God but cannot help a certain preoccupation with the material world.

For most people who struggle with materialism, the deeper problem is that *things* are being trusted *more than God*. People may start out loving God, but anxiety easily takes over when, for example, bankruptcy appears looming or the loss of material assets is at stake. In such a situation, many people grow fearful and worried. They may try to take over, control matters, and "be God" rather than "let go and let God." Instead of surrendering more to prayer, to worship, and to the spiritual solution to which we're called (providing God's answer), people often develop a strictly man-made solution. The focus is more on the problem, one's survival, or the survival of the organization than it is on God. People may even resort to lying, cheating, or stealing to get the money or things they need. The person may be preoccupied with things and with fear and can't trust

God or spend enough time with God in these moments, so they try to fix the problem themselves through a controlling method. Through control, a person can and probably will get the money they're looking for—at least the minimum. However, problems tend to keep repeating themselves until the person discovers how to receive financial blessings. This blessing is in Christ and through God's plan and is God's to give. For those caught in the materialistic mind-set, however, they may often "spin their wheels" until they are willing to surrender spiritually and fully turn their problems over to the care of God.

Too Rich

A far different problem is when a person has already received financial blessings from God. They already have a great deal of money at their disposal. Some of these wealthy say they love God, but at the same time they are in charge of the relationship. They think they're in charge because they've got the money. This can bring the illusion of control. It becomes much harder to surrender to God because, for many of these, they're too attached to their possessions. If God asks them to give up some of their wealth for others, some can't do this adequately because they're too attached to what they have. This was the plight of the rich young man who was invited by Christ to follow him, but was first instructed to sell what he had and give to the poor (Mark 10:21). The passage from Mark indicates that the young man "was saddened, and went away grieving, for he was one who owned much property" (Mark 10:22, NASB). At this, Jesus said to his disciples, "How hard it will be for those who are wealthy to enter the kingdom of God!" (Mark 10:23, NASB). The disciples were shocked at hearing this and said among themselves, "Then who can be saved?" Looking at them, Jesus said, "With people, it is impossible, but not with God; for all things are possible with God." So, then, it's not impossible for the wealthy person to enter the kingdom of God, but that hope rests on their relationship with God alone.

The less attached the wealthy are to their possessions, the easier it will be to share them with others. Many are very generous financially. They have been blessed and they bless others by what they give. This message is not at all to condemn the rich, for there are plenty who share most generously and unselfishly the blessings they've received. It may take some consideration for a person to know whether or not they have a problem with materialism.

All materialism can be changed. Since the change takes place in the heart, through conversion and faith, we should be patient because that takes time. In combating it, I stress the point that the solution is primarily about *trusting God.* Only from the security of that relationship can one detach enough from the world and things to find peace in Christ. To assist us in trusting God, the Virgin Mary has asked us to meditate each Thursday on the following words of Jesus from the Sermon on the Mount:

> You cannot serve both God and mammon (or "money," according to other translations.) Therefore, I tell you, do not worry about your life, what you will eat (or drink), or about your body, what you will wear. Is not life more than food and the body more than clothing? Look at the birds in the sky; they do not sew or reap, they gather nothing into barns, yet your heavenly Father feeds them. Are not you more important than they? Can any of you by worrying add a single moment to your life-span? Why are you anxious about clothes? Learn from the way the wild flowers grow. They do not work or spin. But I tell you that not even Solomon in all his splendor was clothed like one of them. If God so clothes the grass of the field, which grows today and is thrown into the oven tomorrow, will He not much more provide for you, O you of little faith? So do not worry and say 'What are we to eat?' or 'What are we to drink?' or 'What are we to wear?' All these things the pagans seek. Your heavenly Father knows that you need them all. But seek first the

> kingdom of God and His righteousness, and all these
> things will be given to you besides. Do not worry about
> tomorrow; tomorrow will take care of itself. Sufficient
> for a day is its own evil. (Matthew 6:24-34)[105]

Materialism in the Church

Even certain church ministers or ecclesiastical officials have fallen prey to the dangers of materialism. With the church's assets at their disposal, it's possible to lose the focus on God from whom the blessings of this wealth came. If a church pastor or minister disregards Christ's ways in the church, he can lose the blessings and assets that God first gave to the pastor, denomination, ministry, or local church in the first place. If heavy politics take precedence over Christ and the Gospel in that church, those denominations or churches will eventually lose more money and assets than they gain. Just because Christ prophesied that the "gates of hell" would not prevail against the church (Matthew 16:18), that does not mean that an individual church in the United States cannot go bankrupt. It also does not mean that a local church or denomination may not have to close down its operations. It is not only possible. It has happened.

If a local church or denomination is in trouble financially, it is essential to review the policies and practices of such an organization. If they treat people well, reasonably adhere to the Gospel, and pray and worship well, they will prevail and flourish. However, for those who put aside Gospel values out of fear or protection of the organization, such ways will eventually backfire if they consequently hurt God's people. That church will not prevail but will decline. It could even die out. We know from experience that the church or denomination that has flourished has done so when people radically love Jesus Christ and the people to whom he sends us. From this place of worship and Christian love comes every kind of blessing and the solution to even the most vexing problems.

Money and things are not bad in and of themselves. Also, it is not wrong for a person to have wealth. The issue is where a person's *heart* is. What/who does a person love and *trust* more—God or money? I began to see money and things for what they really are—just money and things with no power to make one truly happy or to save one's soul. That is why Jesus puts forth this question in the Gospel: "What will it profit a man if he gains the whole world and forfeits his soul?" (Matthew 16:26, New American Standard Bible) One has a much better chance for a happy soul and an easier path to heaven if God is loved and trusted the most in one's heart. If God is trusted, the man or woman has no need to worry, even in dire circumstances. If a person acts on faith, blessings flow from there. That is why, for example, the Old Testament patriarch Abraham and all his descendants became so blessed. It is because Abraham acted *on faith* (Genesis 22). Likewise, the person who abandons himself to God will not be forsaken but will be heard and helped. The more we do that, the more we'll be able to let go of a financial problem on a spiritual and emotional level. If a person is rich, the more he'll be able to let go of some money for the welfare of others.

If it's an issue, let's make progress against the materialistic mind-set by putting God first in our lives. Let's be reminded again of this promise that's been made by Christ himself: "But seek first the kingdom of God and His righteousness, and all these things shall be given to you besides" (Matthew 6:33).

Not everyone will heed the words of Christ or the message of Medjugorje identified in these previous chapters. For various reasons, there are still many who are not ready to take these matters seriously or who don't want to change. If you tell them of the Medjugorje miracle or the gospel of Jesus, they may say, "that's nice," but then they march to the beat of a different drummer. They may feel too busy to pray or be too interested in other things to pay that much attention to God or to the welfare of their soul. There are also those who simply don't believe. They have little to no faith, and so they doubt whether these spiritual realities even matter. For these and other reasons, I believe prophetic events will take place on the earth. These are mainly for the benefit of those who are slow to believe or who resist practicing conversion. Faith in the unseen is always preferential and will grant a greater reward for those who believe without evidence. However, God wants not just some, but all to be saved. So the next chapter accounts for how the Medjugorje plan will try to draw in those who are waiting rather than converting and those who disbelieve rather than believe. This eighth chapter is the matter of the ten secrets. As the chapter title also indicates, the secrets are also comprised of warnings and chastisement. Don't be alarmed, though, but please read further to understand better what has been revealed and roughly in what time frame we might expect the prophesied events to unfold.

> Dear children! I invite you to decide again to love God above all else. In this time, when due to the spirit of consumerism, one forgets what it means to love and to cherish true values, I invite you again, little children, to put God in the first place in your life. Do not let Satan attract you through material things but, little children, decide for God who is freedom and love. Choose life and not death of the soul, little children, and in this time when you meditate upon the suffering and death of Jesus, I invite you to decide for life which blossomed through the resurrection, and that your life may be renewed today through conversion that shall lead you to eternal life. Thank you for having responded to my call.[106] (March 25, 1996, through the visionary Marija Pavlović-Lunetti, "Monthly Message to the World")

Chapter 8

The Ten Secrets, the Warnings, and the Chastisement

What I address in this chapter concerns the reported inevitability of chastisement. This is probably the most difficult part of the Medjugorje message and one major reason why I think the Church evaluates Medjugorje cautiously. I am not a doomsayer and I don't think it's the end of the world. I am simply a messenger in this regard and only report that which others (the visionaries) have said is true. I've read about six books and several periodicals on this topic, and they've all more or less described the same or very similar warnings contained within the secrets. To explain this better, I'll use the journalist Wayne Weible's 1986 publication *Miracle at Medjugorje* and the book *Words from Heaven* (St. James Publishing, 1996). The visionaries base everything in this regard on what the Virgin Mary has reportedly disclosed to them. I'll present this as accurately as I can for your discernment. Though prophecies can be imperfect, we should consider that six people have given a lengthy witness to the nature of these secrets and warnings. Six people have yet to be disproven after every kind of test conceivable (refer to appendix 2 for tests on the visionaries). We must consider the real possibility—six people may be telling us the truth. The purpose of this information is not to scare people. In 365 locations in the Bible, we'll find these or similar words: do not be afraid. I believe the secrets are not meant to scare, but to prepare. If we're not prepared when the secrets come to pass, then at that future point, it's probably time to be afraid. In the Bible, it's written, "The fear of the Lord is the beginning of all wisdom" (Proverbs 9:10, NIV). So, which is it? Should we be afraid or not? People who worship God and who live according to his Word don't have anything to be afraid of. On the other hand, if the fear of God leads someone to relationship with the Lord and improving one's ways, that fear is not a bad thing. To maintain some fear of God is advisable for anyone. "And his mercy is upon generation after generation toward those who fear him" (Luke 1:50, NASB). As we get to know God's love, however, we have all the more reason to heed his words, "be not afraid" (Genesis 46:3, NIV).

Introduction to the Ten Secrets

Warnings of chastisement are contained within the so-called *ten secrets,* which the Blessed Mother has given or will give to each of the six visionaries. Nobody, *except the visionaries,* knows what the secrets are since Mary has instructed the seers not to tell anyone about the content. That's why they're called secrets. When questioned about the secrets in public, the visionary Ivan lightly reminds people, "I cannot say anything about the secrets because they are secrets!" However, there is some limited information the visionaries have been permitted to share about the ten secrets. First, they are not all *negative* events or chastisements. There are some positive events included in the ten secrets. For example, a sign has been promised by Mary on the hill called Podbrdo in Medjugorje. It will be physical, permanent, and indestructible. It will be possible to photograph it, according to the visionaries. This sign, also referred to as the Great Sign, will serve as testimony and proof that the Blessed Mother has been appearing in Medjugorje.

We should not wait for the appearance of this sign before we begin our individual conversion! The question is will it be too late for people to *begin* their conversion by that point? It will be too late if you were given some faith before the sign's appearance but did not act on it: "Be converted! It will be too late when the sign comes. Beforehand, several warnings will be given to the world. Hurry to be converted. I need your prayers and your penance" [107] (Blessed Virgin Mary, April 25, 1983). If it will be too late for conversion when the sign comes, one might reasonably ask then why would God send the sign? As I understand it, this physical sign is mainly for atheists. It is mainly to provide sufficient evidence to atheists that God exists, with the hope of saving their souls.

Those whose faith is weak may be encouraged by the promise of warnings to take place before the Great Sign comes. These are referred to by Mary in the quote just cited, April 25, 1983. These warnings will be the first of the ten secrets to occur. They will confirm the presence and message of Mary at Medjugorje and are meant to spur on those who had been waiting to begin hastening their conversion. One takes a chance by waiting for these to pass since we don't know what will happen or where. We must also understand that individual conversion can take a long time. The visionary Mirjana Dragićević-Soldo has a special role in communicating the secrets, and she will witness them in her lifetime, according to the Virgin's own words. "Before the visible sign is given to humanity, there will be three warnings to the world. The warnings will be warnings on the earth. Mirjana will witness them." [108] Now in 2012, Mirjana is forty-seven years old.

The first event or secret does not sound good:

> "Our Lady showed Mirjana the first secret—the earth was desolate (quoting Mary):
>
> It is the upheaval of a region of the world. In the world there are so many sins. What can I do, if you do not help me? Remember that I love you. God does not have a hard heart. Look around you and see what men do.

Then you will no longer say that God has a hard heart. How many people come to church, to the house of God, with respect, a strong faith, and love God? Very few! Here you have a time of grace and conversion. It is necessary to use it well." [109]

Regarding the other secrets, we also know that the ninth and tenth are chastisements, and we know that the tenth is the most serious of all the secrets. It has been said by Mirjana that the tenth secret cannot be eliminated because "we cannot expect the conversion of the whole world." [110] The seventh secret, which was also a chastisement, has been eliminated. Mirjana reported that it was canceled in response to prayer and fasting.

We're also told that the ten secrets are *not all* events relating to the *whole world*. Actually, it's been reported that only four of the secrets relate to the wider world. The others relate to the individual lives of the six visionaries and the territory of Medjugorje: "While the content of none of the secrets is yet known, the seers say that only four of the revelations are common to all mankind; the others have to do with the individual visionaries or the Medjugorje community." [111]

Regarding chastisement, what strikes me is that the ten secrets have not even begun yet. *None* of the difficult events that have already taken place in the world had reference to the ten secrets of Medjugorje. The ten secrets are still in the future. They will not begin, according to Mirjana, until all six visionaries have received all ten secrets. To this day, only three visionaries have received all ten secrets (Mirjana, Ivanka, and Jakov). The other three visionaries have received nine out of ten secrets (Ivan, Vicka, and Marija). The last one to receive the tenth secret was Jakov on September 12, 1998. The next previous one to receive the tenth secret was Ivanka on May 6, 1985. The first one to receive the tenth secret was Mirjana on December 25, 1982.

Consistent with the Bible

The nature of apocalyptic events is consistent with the Bible. Jesus predicted catastrophes to take place before his Second Coming in glory. While catastrophe is not what Medjugorje is about, we must nonetheless consider the significance and meaning of catastrophe. Jesus referred to events like earthquakes, famines, nation rising against nation and kingdom against kingdom. These were described by him as the "beginning of the birth pangs." [112] What I believe he means are the pains to be endured by the peoples and parts of the world in preparation for that time when he will return in glory "on the clouds of heaven." [113] At that time, all will be judged and sent to their eternal destination (according to chapter 25 of the Gospel according to Matthew).

Those who are choosing not to follow in God's ways should repent, lest they risk the wrath that is foretold. Jesus continues, "For as the days of Noah were, so will be the coming of the Son of Man. For as in those days before the flood they were eating and drinking, marrying and giving in marriage, until the day Noah entered the ark, and they knew nothing until the flood came and swept them all away, so too will be the coming of the Son of Man. Then two will be in the field; one will be taken and one will be left. Two women will be grinding meal together; one will be taken and one will be left. Keep awake therefore, for you do not know on what day your Lord is coming." [114]

Modern-Day Perspective

As we consider all the wars, famines, and natural disasters since the beginning of the twentieth century until now, it seems to me that these difficult biblical prophecies have begun, and we continue through this stressful period on the earth. A terrible famine took place, escalating in 2011, in Somalia, a country located in the Horn of Africa. Though the United Nations reported that the famine has ended, they also indicated that the area remains quite vulnerable and that the crisis there is not over. We know that Africa, especially, has suffered the great pain of famine before this one in recent decades. Many will remember the terrible famine in Ethiopia and Eritrea during the 1980's that led to some 400,000 deaths. In the recent twenty years, how many floods, tornadoes, earthquakes, hurricanes, even tsunamis have we heard about? A recent tsunami and earthquake on Japan's coast took at least eighteen thousand lives in 2011, causing untold damage. The United States has experienced a great deal of flooding during the last ten years, especially from 2008-2011. Hurricane Irene caused a great deal of damage and flooding along the East Coast of the USA in August 2011, causing destruction from North Carolina all the way up to Vermont. Tornadoes have also stepped up in the States, most recently devastating the town of Joplin, Missouri, in early 2011. A number of other states have experienced significant destruction of property from tornadoes in recent years. Many serious hurricanes hit Florida and the South of the USA in recent years, although Florida seems to have been spared of serious hurricanes during the last four to five years or so. Hurricane Katrina in New Orleans, Louisiana was a devastating storm in 2005, and people from that area are still recovering. A very strong earthquake in Pakistan during 2005 killed at least seventy thousand people. The small island of Haiti has experienced untold damage as a result of their many storms, hurricanes, and a terrible earthquake in 2010 which claimed 300,000 lives, injured many more, and caused massive destruction of property.

Many fail to see or understand these signs of the times. They might pass it off as global warming, El Nino, or La Nina. These are names for meteorological trends. They may rationalize it as some other natural or scientific incident. However, there is usually a spiritual dimension to these disorders also. That is not to mean we should understand God as an angry, vengeful God who is saying, "Take that!" In my opinion, chaotic or violent disruptions in the natural environment are not caused by God. Obviously, God allows natural disasters to take place, though. I don't know why he allows those things to occur. However, I think that, the more that people stray from the ways of God or reject God, the more these things tend to happen. I don't like referring to natural disasters as "acts of God" the way some insurance companies do. God has ultimate dominion over everything that happens, yes. However, I don't believe he wants any of this destruction to take place, the likes of which the world has seen. He allows it because he allows free will. It's my opinion that nature corrects and restores the earth's balance. Such balance goes into disarray due to multiple and complex factors. These I cannot explain fully, but I believe an important part of that disorder is the aggregate, cumulative effect of human acts against nature. These happen every day and are many and varied. So, I will not go into detail on that topic.

Another factor that causes disorder is occult worship. When occult worship is tolerated in a particular place, such people invite other powers to affect the environment. These forces are not imaginary but real, and when invited, they can tamper with nature. If there's some kind of natural disaster, it's very hard to identify what the causes are, and many times it's not possible to prove anything more than natural causes. Yet, due to the increased severity and multiplicity of such events on earth, we must consider why nature has reacted so violently in numerous cases. Who can fully grasp this mystery? God alone is able.

There is a God at work, who is always working toward the good, and there is evil at work which causes the opposite. I'm not God and I'm not a meteorologist. So, I can't take a look at the Japan tsunami, for example, and say what the causes were. Something was clearly is great disorder. Causing the earthquake and sending waves to crash in on people and kill them has nothing to do with the works of God. Like many disasters, it seems to point to a significant pressure on the earth caused by either a great excess of something and/or a great lack of something else. Eventually, the earth gives way. Perhaps in some way, disasters like these could be analogized to a balloon which fills up with too much air. Eventually, the balloon explodes.

If smoke fills a room, people will eventually start coughing. If greenhouse gases and other fumes and smoke are released in the air, what do we think happens with all that? Do they just go away? When there's too much of something bad or not enough of something good, something eventually gives way. Natural laws do what they must to deal with all the pressures and forces. It is corrective to create balance in the environment. Sir Isaac Newton said, "For every action, there is an equal and opposite reaction." Certainly, those laws apply in this regard. Does the devil get his hand in the mix and make bad or disordered situations worse? My opinion is sometimes yes, but it seems impossible to prove and make any kind of judgments on how the powers of darkness work in particular situations. I think, in short, they like to go where there's trouble and make it worse. I recently asked a woman in my church why she thought there'd been so many natural disasters in the modern era. She simply answered, "Sin." Again, it's hard to make judgments and direct correlations in this regard. However, many sins do open the door to disorders on the earth. The enemy is happy to take disorder and turn it into chaos or disaster.

Can God come in and fix all the disorders that exist? I believe that God can do anything, but it would seem like enabling if he just came in to pick up the pieces every time things fell out of order. He can protect people from every kind of disaster the nature of which I've already described. I believe God has done this many times and has averted many a disaster in the world. He does this on account of love and, when his love and help are accepted and welcomed, he will come to our aid. On account of the same love, he respects free-will and will not force himself or his help on people. So, he's not going to just impose himself and just fix everything all the time. This is even though he would really like to and help his sons and daughters avoid every kind of calamity. But he always leaves us to choose for or against him. God is saddened when people choose to go their own way and be apart from him. God is likewise saddened to witness the trouble man can bring upon himself or others by his actions or behavior. The Lord is pleased when his sons and daughters accept him and permit him to bless our lives, to order our world, and to be recognized and acknowledged everywhere. Is that happening? We have to look at the way our society relates to God. If a prayer cannot be said at a public school or graduation ceremony or if the Ten Commandments can't be displayed in a public building, what does this mean? After 9-11, we had half the country displaying signs that said, "God bless America" and nobody seemed to be complaining about that then. How quickly we forget.

Meaning of Chastisements

The warnings of chastisement communicated through Medjugorje are not intended to create anxiety but are mentioned to make people aware of the significance of the times in which we live. Chastisement, however, is *not* what the message of Medjugorje is about, and it is not what the Blessed Mother wants us to be thinking about. Ivan reports in public talks that Our Lady has not come to talk about the end of the world. The Mother of God's intention is to lead us to *peace*, not to anxiety about future disaster. Yet she mentions the reality the world faces (if it continues on its present path) in order that we may avert chastisement as much as possible.

I do not think much about chastisements, and that is what I believe God wants. When one thinks about the Virgin Mary and Medjugorje, the last connection that should be in the person's mind is the thought of chastisement. That is because Medjugorje is the opposite of what chastisement is about. To quote the late Father Slavko Barbaric, a Franciscan parish priest who served the parish in Medjugorje, "Regarding the question of an apocalyptic dimension, certainly, we understand the possibility for catastrophe to occur. But the Blessed Mother did not come primarily to speak about catastrophes; she came to show us the way to peace. Those who see Medjugorje primarily from an apocalyptic point of view have not really grasped where she is trying to lead us." [115]

Medjugorje is a peace plan, not a destruction plan. As I hope you'll agree from reading this chapter, punishment or chastisements are consequences when heaven's call to repentance and conversion fails. However, we should not let chastisement become our focus because that perspective is likely to cause distress. When I returned home from my first Medjugorje trip in 1988, I recall some anxiety about the potential for future destruction because I had just begun to learn about the ten secrets. As I looked at skyscrapers, I wondered whether I might someday see a few of them fall down. Of course, none of that brought me any peace. Realizing this, and discovering that these were not things the Virgin Mary wanted me to be thinking about, I found a way to get such things out of my mind. I considered more serene thoughts and found more peace by praying the rosary or reading the Bible.

I do not believe that God is about death, disaster, or destruction, but about life, creation, rebirth, and re-creation. Let me cite the aftermath of Hurricane Katrina as an example. I saw Christ not in the destruction but in the rebuilding of this area and the enormous outpouring of charity to those who lost so much. The negative things that happen are not what God is about. God loves us deeply and does not wish people harm. Before we blame God, we should consider other possible causes for things that go wrong: (1) human beings, individually or as a group of people and society and (2) the influence and effect of evil. In explaining this, the following paragraphs may seem unpleasant, but they contain a dose of reality that is good to confront.

Let's start with the view that man causes harm by his own actions. Certain actions are *self-destructive*. Wrongful behavior may have, if not amended, a causal effect on future troubles that take place. Historically, whether one considers the fall of the Roman Empire, the fall of Saddam Hussein, Egypt's Hosni Mubarak, President Richard Nixon, the debacle involving the company Solyndra, the collapse of the company Enron, or the 2008 collapse of the US banking and mortgage system, was it not human errors or corruption that brought on the declines and disasters? Too quickly, people blame God and point to God when disaster strikes and then they get angry at God. We should consider what humankind has done or what society has done to contribute to whatever crisis we may be facing.

Another major problem remains widespread and it is also self-destructive. This is abortion throughout the world. Many have become so habituated to having abortion legal and on demand that they have become desensitized to its ill effects. Do not *over 30 million abortions* in the United States alone since 1973 signal something seriously wrong? Abortion is an act that not only terminates the life of the unborn but has also harmed the hearts and souls of the women who have aborted, not to mention the fathers of these children. These acts are forgivable, but first there must be repentance and sorrow for these actions. It's possible for the woman or the man (if he was also complicit) to be brought to a place of forgiveness and peace.

I also cited the influence and effect of evil as a second reason why things go wrong. I'm stressing this not to give the devil undue attention, but mainly to stress that an ongoing battle rages between heaven and hell and human souls are at stake. Our Lady explained this to the visionaries early on in the apparitions: "A great struggle is about to unfold. A struggle between my Son and Satan. Human souls are at stake" (A Friend of Medjugorje, *Words from Heaven*, p.96). The devil, Lucifer, was once a high-ranking angel in heaven. Supremely intelligent, he later became arrogant and rebellious. Subsequently, he was kicked out of heaven for failing to give due worship to God. He been raising hell, if you will, ever since and been trying to drag everyone else down into his pit. For mysterious reasons, evil is permitted to co-exist along with the good and we have a choice as to whom we cooperate with. As mentioned in chapter 6, the work of the devil is real and has been acknowledged by Our Lady of Medjugorje many times. Evil is authored and initiated by the devil, also referred to in the Bible as Satan. His existence is acknowledged by Jesus: "Then He (Jesus) will say to those on his left, 'Depart from me, you accursed, into the eternal fire prepared *for the devil and his angels*'" (emphasis mine) (Matthew 25:41).[116] Demons are coconspirators with the devil and include fallen angels that are sent to wander the earth, looking to create disorder, pain, hatred, bitterness, hostility, chaos, confusion, trouble, destruction, fear, and terror, not to mention other evils. Essentially, their work is basically to turn upside down and inside out the plans and the goodness of God in individual people, the church, and the world. Wherever God plants goodness and beauty, they want to twist that into the opposite. Why? It is simply because they hate God. They can't get to Jesus so they go after us. Allow me to cite a few examples in the paragraphs to follow.

Was not twenty-two-year-old Jared Lee Loughner overtaken by the devil when he shot US congresswoman Gabrielle Giffords on January 8, 2011, in Tucson, Arizona? He shot nineteen people that day, six of them fatally. One of those killed was U.S. District Court Judge John Roll. Miraculously, congresswoman Giffords survived a gunshot wound to the head and continues her impressive recovery.

There have been similar violent attacks in recent years. Was not the young student at Virginia Tech, Seung-Hui Cho, being motivated by the demonic realm when he went on a shooting spree and killed thirty-two of his fellow college students in April 2007? In 2012, we've just heard of a terribly violent act which took place in a movie theater in Aurora, Colorado. Twenty-four year old James Holmes walked into the theater armed with guns and shot dozens of people who were there to see the new *Batman* movie. The latest death toll stands at twelve and the number injured is fifty-eight at the time this chapter was completed. I'm not convinced that mental illness alone is enough to explain such rampant, wanton, and violent acts.

Cho concluded the violence by killing himself, but Loughner and Holmes remain alive. At his arraignment, prosecutors charged James

Holmes with twenty-four counts of murder and one hundred and sixteen counts of attempted murder. (There were two different counts cited for each death and for each injured person.) Jared Loughner and his attorney struck a plea bargain agreement at a hearing in August, 2012. By this time, Loughner had been found competent to stand trial. He pled guilty to nineteen counts of murder or attempted murder and formal sentencing is scheduled for November 2012. It has been agreed that this sentence will be life imprisonment without the possibility of parole. As part of this plea deal, prosecutors will not seek the death penalty.

Such tragedies don't just happen indiscriminately and by chance. We must be attuned to all strange human behavior and odd spiritual or occult practices which are evident beforehand. Investigators found an idol skull in a tent in the backyard of Jared Loughner. It was on an altar set up with candles, so there's some significant evidence of satanic or occult worship. That welcomes the demonic to enter someone's psyche. If demons successfully enter someone, it requires deliverance or an exorcism to get them out. I address those issues in chapter 6. This becomes complex, but the point is that God had nothing to do with these evils. Obviously, we had very troubled and disturbed young people with some grave psychological problems. The enemy knows who is disturbed on a human level, and if that person's mind and heart welcome the ploys and lies of Satan, whether knowingly or unknowingly, then this person can do some serious harm. We should know that evil is the author of such terrible things.

Thus far in this chapter, it may sound like I'm saying God never has a role in causing difficult things to take place in our personal lives or in society. That is not true and it would be overly simplistic to say so. There are places in the Bible where you can find evidence that God has punished sin and intentionally sent affliction as discipline. It takes a discerning mind to know when trouble is from God. One general rule is that God acts fairly and the devil doesn't. If we consider Medjugorje, just consider how much time and how patiently heaven has been working to help us avoid trouble. Then, compare that with the sudden and wanton recklessness of the Loughner, Cho, and Holmes incidents. Without warning and in an extremely violent fashion, innocent people are killed or injured by another person. This is completely unfair to people who were the unfortunate victims of being in the wrong place at the wrong time.

Can calamity ever be traced to God's own orders? In limited circumstances, disaster can occur directly on account of "the wrath of God." If a certain wrath is sent by God, it's only to serve a higher good. Otherwise, God would not permit it to happen. We know from the book of Revelation, for example, that God will exercise wrath against his enemies in the last times. Angels from heaven are appointed to execute God's wrath on the earth:

> The smoke of the incense along with the prayers of the holy ones went up before God from the hand of the angel . . . The seven angels who were holding the seven trumpets prepared to blow them. When the first one blew his trumpet, there came hail and fire mixed with blood, which was hurled down to the earth. A third of the land was burned up, along with a third of the trees and all green grass.[117]

It doesn't sound like a pretty picture, does it? Why would a loving God execute such wrath? Sometimes, God has to execute wrath because it's no longer possible in such cases for goodness, peace, and order to flourish without wiping out the evil first. In such a case, the evil has developed such a powerful stronghold that God has to send wrath as a last resort and means by which to ultimately restore and recreate goodness. That being the case, Revelation also tells us that God will even create a new earth: "Then I saw a new heaven and a new earth. The former heaven and the former earth had passed away, and the sea was no more."[118] That, however, concerns the end of the world. Can God's wrath be exercised before that? I believe that, yes, it can, but for the same reason described in the earlier part of this paragraph.

I would like to end this chapter on more positive footing. As I began the chapter, we are instructed not to be afraid. That instruction applies to all of the difficult things covered in this chapter. God's people should not be afraid. Those who love God, worship him, and do their best to follow in his ways have the assurance of his protection. This chapter was mainly intended to address the ten secrets. Since some of the secrets are described as difficult events or chastisements, I also tried to explain in this chapter that such calamity is not what God wants. What God wants is our conversion. Disaster or calamity is something Mary has been trying to help us avert, but at the present stage we must be prepared to expect that many of us will witness at least some of these events in future years. There is no reason to believe that their severity cannot be mitigated further by heeding the Word of God and by responding to recommendations of the Virgin Mary.

The next two chapters were written in order to address moral theology. I wrote those chapters because historical Judeo-Christian faith is based on divine revelation and we are being reminded of these truths through Medjugorje. Beginning with the Old Testament, we have written accounts of how God guided and instructed humankind to behave, beginning with Adam and Eve. Further on, God gave the Ten Commandments through Moses. The law is fulfilled and brought to perfection through the life, teachings, and example of Jesus. Without grasping this fundamental background of Judeo-Christian morality and history, the Medjugorje messages and prophetic warnings would make far less sense. However, if we understand the theology and how much God has helped to guide, shepherd, and teach his people, it puts the entire prophetic revelation of Medjugorje in much better context. I conclude this very challenging chapter with Our Lady's words, directing us to the word of God.

Dear children, put Sacred Scripture in a visible place in your family and read it. In this way, you will come to know prayer with the heart and your thoughts will be on God. Do not forget that you are passing like a flower in the field, which is visible from afar but disappears in a moment. Little children, leave a sign of goodness and love wherever you pass and God will bless you with an abundance of His blessing. Thank you for having responded to my call.[119] (The Blessed Virgin Mary's Message to the World, January 25, 2007, through the visionary Marija Pavlović-Lunetti)

Chapter 9

Moral Theology, Sin, and Their Biblical Foundations

Since the previous chapter addressed the topic of chastisement, I've chosen to segue to this chapter with the discussion of another challenging topic: sin. It's important to take a look at the meaning of sin because it would make no sense why God would send warnings of chastisement without understanding what behaviors or actions would warrant such warnings or future consequences in the first place. The previous chapter described the nature of some warnings that were predicted at Medjugorje. This chapter will describe the behaviors that make warnings and the possibility for chastisement necessary. I will also try to establish a theological and biblical foundation for sin.

What Is Sin?

Many people will not understand chastisement because many people don't understand *sin*. Many people think they have no sin, and often, it's the same people who do not see or understand sin in their surrounding culture. For many, everything has become "okay," or many young people say to so many things, "That's cool." Recently, I heard a priest preaching at St. James Church, the Medjugorje parish.

He said one of the devil's most common lies is that a certain action isn't wrong because *everybody else is doing it.* We need to be careful what we define as "okay," "cool," or acceptable behavior regardless of what everybody else is doing. The activities we thought were harmless may be much more harmful than we think.

Sin is not a popular word and many people would rather exclude it from their dictionary. If we understood though that it is out of love and a desire to protect us that God defines sin, the same people may not think so negatively about this word. At this point, I would like to provide a brief fundamental teaching about sin, with reference to its basic, underlying, and biblical foundation. Again, I don't expect a Justin Bieber-like fan reaction by raising this topic. This chapter and the next will focus on what are right and wrong behaviors. For some, this will be eye-opening and it will be hard to read some of it. For others, these chapters (nine and ten) will only be reminders or confirmations of what you already believe.

Where Did We Get the Concept of Sin?

The word "sin" has no meaning unless it is related to God. Neither you nor I are the final arbiters of right and wrong, good and evil. That's because we didn't create human nature, and we didn't create the world and the natural environment in which we live. God did. Having the wisdom of knowing best what he made and how he made it, he is the best judge of right and wrong and what is good and bad. As such, the compass by which to identify sin is the Word of God as found in the Bible. I would define sin as follows: *an action or omission of activity that deliberately and knowingly breaks the law of God and that is a course of action or inaction chosen freely.*

It's on this foundation that I would say there *is* an *objective moral truth* defined by God that is common to all men and women. There is room for exceptions in these matters based on justifiable circumstances. That does not erase, however, the fact that there are certain actions that are objectively evil by their very nature. An example is murder. The fifth commandment is "Thou shalt not kill." God communicated this commandment, along with all of the Ten Commandments through Moses.[120] However, we cannot always say that the person who commits murder is always morally culpable and therefore guilty of crime or moral judgment. Exceptions exist when a person kills as an act of self-defense against the violent and life-threatening actions of another. Other exceptions relate to acts of war. The justifiable actions of a law enforcement officer may also exempt one from crime or moral judgment. In general though, we know that it a serious evil to kill someone in almost all circumstances.

The Ten Commandments are written in the book of Exodus (chapter 20, verses 1-17). God wanted these to be so clear that he actually printed them on stone tablets. "When the Lord finished speaking to Moses on Mount Sinai, he gave him the two tablets of the covenant law, the tablets of stone inscribed by the finger of God" (Exodus 31:18, New International Version). If we break one of these commandments, then—unless we can be excused by justifiable circumstances—we've committed a sin. That's because these are *commandments,* not suggestions or recommendations. Especially with these ten matters, God is very clear, and we should be able to understand them. If we can figure out a TV weather report and we can understand the headlines on the front page of the newspaper, we can understand the Ten Commandments. "Thou shalt not steal," [121] for example, is a straightforward concept that people grasp quite easily. This is the seventh commandment. If we steal money from someone's wallet, then we've broken a commandment. Unless there's some way to justify taking the money, we've committed a sin against God and against that person. "Honor your father and mother" [122] is the fourth commandment. If we act dishonorably toward parents, then we've broken the fourth commandment. Children hurt their parents and will usually break the fourth commandment if they refuse, out of anger or some other reason, to communicate with their parents. If Christmas is observed in the family, it would be wrong for someone not to at least send a card or gift if they will not be with their parent(s) in person. In serious circumstances, a person may be justified in choosing not to communicate with a parent for an extended period. When there has been violence or serious abuse, it would be understandable. In such an unfortunate case, one could still work on the relationship through a written letter. The person might also consider calling if someone else could be on speaker-phone to support them. They might also arrange to see the parent in person during a family get together since other people will be around.

Refusing to communicate would also be wrong of the parent toward their child. It is equally wrong for a parent to refuse to communicate with their own child, also excepting serious circumstances. In fact, the parent could be more culpable and at fault for an ongoing rift if the child is not mature or old enough to know how to work on the relationship himself.

In family relationships, especially, the goal should always be to reconcile. However, one person cannot force the other to reconcile if the other chooses not to. In such a circumstance, the best that a person can do is to forgive the other person and to pray for them to ease up and start talking again. We are always called to forgiveness, which is a healing process within ourselves. To *reconcile*, however, requires the cooperation of both parties to resume the relationship. We should strive for this, but again, we cannot force it to happen. Some people, when upset at someone, like to use the silent treatment. If the relationship is to survive, somebody has to be the better man (or woman) and eventually say something to the one who will not speak. I've been in this awkward position numerous times. I've succeeded in ending the silent treatment many times by simply asking the other person a question or by talking about the weather. I can't remember a time when the other person did not say something back. That's probably because they really didn't want the silence to continue either.

Lost

There has been a show on TV in the recent past called *Lost*. I would likewise use the term to describe the understanding some people have today with regard to the topic of sin. Many people of this world are *lost* in a belief system in which they either see no sin or they see it only in the most serious or extreme circumstances like murder. There is much more to the picture of sin than this. If anyone believes he has no sin, that person has been deceived, according to St. John:

"If we say, 'We are without sin,' we deceive ourselves, and the truth is not in us" (1 John 1:8).[123] Likewise, St. Paul says, "All have sinned and fall short of the glory of God" (Romans 3:23).[124]

So to understand the warning of chastisement, it's important to recognize that all have sinned. Despite the mercy of God, which is great, the visionary Mirjana Dragićević-Soldo has revealed that we must expect some measure of chastisement to come. This is because the Blessed Virgin revealed to her that we cannot expect the conversion of the whole world. Since I'm making a connection between sin and chastisement, you might infer that God sometimes chooses to punish people. It is true, but we really should not be too surprised about it. Anyone who has been a parent knows that a child needs discipline and that it is even necessary sometimes to punish the child. Even if you are not a parent, it is just common sense that the threat of punishment or the punishment itself is sometimes a necessary deterrent or disciplinary action in relation to wrong behavior. It is very similar with the Lord and the manner in which he relates to us, his sons and daughters. If we are punished or given some penance, it is always out of love and concern that God allows this to happen. If our parents didn't pay attention to us growing up, and gave us a carte blanche to do whatever we wanted, how much would we have felt loved? We would have developed the sense that they didn't care. By analogy, the threat of chastisement or even the chastisement itself should signal that God cares about us. He cares about the quality of our life on earth and cares about where we go after death. We should remember in this context that unrepented sin carries much greater consequences in terms of penalties than repented sin. We could analogize two people who get pulled over for speeding. The first apologizes to the officer and explains that he's late for work and that it won't happen again. He gets a warning. The officer asks the second one what happened and he says that he hasn't done anything wrong because people speed on this highway all the time. The officer gives him a speeding ticket and a $300 fine. People who don't repent aren't trying to change their ways while those who are truly repentant are sorry and are trying to convert. I believe the chastisement foretold has more to do with unrepentant sin.

Any discussion of chastisement should take place alongside a discussion of mercy because God is both merciful and just. Mercy comes in abundance because of Jesus who sets us free from guilt and sin. The blood he shed atones for *all of our sins*. We need to claim that victory in our lives. If we believe ourselves to be in some sin, it's essential to ask Jesus to forgive us, to be sorry for the wrongdoing, and claim his saving death as our salvation. Then we can have peace and be in his grace. If you believe yourself to be in some sin, consider saying sincerely this prayer:

Prayer of Repentance

(Pause for a moment of silence)

Lord Jesus Christ, you died a painful death on a cross to save my soul, and you rose from the dead on the third day. You have saved my life from destruction. Merciful Jesus, I am truly sorry for all my sins. Please forgive me. I didn't mean to hurt you. Come into my heart. Cleanse me of my sin. Renew and save my life. I choose you. Heal my soul. Change my life. Rescue me. I choose you this day as my Lord and Savior. I claim your blood as my saving redemption.

Thank you, Lord Jesus. I praise your holy name. Walk with me, Lord. I need you. I love you. Jesus I trust in you. Amen.

Let's not get discouraged or despair if we've committed some sins, even a large number of sins. Welcome to the human race! If there's some sin, let's repent of any wrong behaviors and claim the victory Christ won by dying on the cross and rising from the dead! If we do, we will *rise with him* and *overcome* sin in our lives. We may fall a number of times along the path of our conversion from sin, but as long as we keep coming back with contrition, asking Jesus to pardon our offenses, we'll be forgiven and saved. In this capacity, we must recognize that Jesus is not just a man who was crucified or who was just a prophet. My faith is that *Jesus is God*, the Lord, and after he was crucified, he rose from the dead. The New Testament accounts for some five hundred people who saw Jesus alive and resurrected following his death on the cross. Such accounts can be found in the Gospels of Matthew, Luke, and John, as well as in the Acts of the Apostles. In his baptism of blood, he paid for all our sins, no matter how many they may be. In his resurrection, we go from death to life. "If you confess with your mouth that Jesus is Lord and believe in your heart that God raised Him from the dead, you will be saved"[125] (Romans 10:9).

Recognizing one's own fault, repenting, and believing firmly in Jesus are the best things we can do for ourselves and for those with whom we're in relationship, including God. Catholics are invited to confession because that sacrament has been given to us. This is also called the sacrament of reconciliation. Our Lady of Medjugorje asks us to avail ourselves of this sacrament once a month. The church believes it is Christ himself forgiving in sacramental confession, speaking and acting through the priest who is his anointed representative on earth. If one is not Catholic, that person should follow the dictates of their own faith, the practice of their church or denomination, and their conscience in making their repentance. Other Christian faiths also value a confession of sin to another person. This is in accord with the Bible, where it is written,

"Confess your sins to one another and pray for one another so that you may be healed" (James 5:16).

This chapter on moral theology has included a review of the fourth, fifth, and seventh commandments in practical applications. The next chapter, on the topic of divine justice, also explores the third and the sixth commandments, while also commenting further on the fifth. Medjugorje reveals God's love. Within such love, laws must exist to give us a compass by which to live and an indication of what is expected. One important way by which we show our love for God is by respecting his will and precepts. Because violations of his commandments can harm ourselves, others, or society, there must be consequences for wrong behavior. Thus, the next chapter continues with a discussion on divine justice alongside a consideration of some other commandments.

> Dear children, God the Father is sending me to show you the way of salvation because He, my children, desires to save you and not to condemn you. That is why I, as a mother, am gathering you around me, because with my motherly love I desire to help you to be free of the dirtiness of the past and to begin to live anew and differently. I am calling you to resurrect in my Son. Along with confession of sins renounce everything that has distanced you from my Son and that has made your life empty and unsuccessful. Say "yes" to the Father with the heart and set out on the way of salvation to which He is calling you through the Holy Spirit. Thank you. I am especially praying for the shepherds, for God to help them to be alongside you with a fullness of heart. (The Blessed Virgin Mary's message given through the visionary Mirjana Dragićević-Soldo at Medjugorje, May 2, 2011) [126]

Chapter 10

God and Justice

In the context of Medjugorje, I want to continue addressing issues of morality while exploring the issue of justice. We can avert much of the chastisement foretold and future troubles by curtailing and converting from behaviors which are hurting ourselves or our society. Some people have failed to understand divine justice and that God administers or allows justice when people do not respond to his love, mercy, and calls to conversion and repentance. The heart of God is mercy and we continue to live in a time of much mercy. But without justice, things would become chaotic because there would be no deterrent, no consequences by which to discipline bad behavior. Many people would basically do whatever they felt like doing. So, mercy must live alongside justice. Justice is built into society, is within natural laws, human rules of conduct, and other ways that our behavior and relationships are treated fairly and equitably. Other times, justice takes place within a person, as his nature or soul is affected by behavior that he had chosen. More broadly, when a whole society goes against the ways of God, this creates a more widespread need for justice. In his permissive will, God allows difficult things to take place on the earth in response to bad behaviors, but only so that good may eventually come about. Even in God's justice there is mercy and he afflicts only to heal.

The discussion of justice should not make us lose sight that God is slow to anger, very merciful and patient. With the Medjugorje event, mercy is shown by the fact that people are being given time to change, and we will be given sufficient opportunity to follow the ways of God. The phenomenon has been going on for thirty-one years, and there is still time for conversion. The Medjugorje event has ushered in a time of particular grace. This is a sign of God's mercy despite much godlessness in this world. One sign of godlessness is that over *30 million babies* have been aborted in the USA alone since 1973. The mystery of justice results in difficulties or consequences if there is no repentance or change. Justice repairs and makes amends for the damage that one's mistakes cause to others, to oneself, and to God. It may hurt at the time, but that same suffering produces greater character and a much better perspective on what is important in life.

Forgiveness and mercy can always mitigate and ease the pains of justice or chastisement. To miss that point would be to miss what Christ accomplished on the cross. Christ showed his love when he chose to suffer a torturous death and be crucified. He paid the price for all of our sins. He paid our sin debt *in full*. I'm certainly not encouraging this, but nobody should despair even if they've committed the same sin one thousand times. You cannot say that even this number is beyond forgiveness. In the New Testament, the apostle Peter asks Jesus how many times he should forgive his brother. Peter asks if up to seven times is adequate. Jesus replies that he should forgive not seven times, but seventy times seven times (Matthew 18:20-22, NASB). From this statement, it can be inferred that we should set no limits on how many times we forgive someone for wrong action. This is because the Lord has no number limit on how many of our own sins he's willing to forgive. We cannot measure this because the mercy of God that comes to us in Christ is infinite and without measure.

A truly repentant sinner who comes to God with contrition and sorrow for sin, and who asks to be forgiven, will be forgiven. At the same time, the forgiveness process isn't meant to be like a washing machine to which we keep returning to clean dirty clothes. We'll be converted with great difficulty and only very slowly if we have that habit and attitude. At the same time, nobody should despair if the number of falls is so great that we think it's beyond God's mercy to keep being forgiven. We must accept what he's done and plead that his blood washes away all our sins. Others may despair if they think the gravity of a single sin or group of sins is so great that they can't be forgiven. I recommend watching a dvd of *The Passion of the Christ.* While watching this film, the same person should be able to answer the question: is his suffering and blood enough to wash away my guilt? A problem is that many people have still not accepted God's forgiveness. We can't pay off a debt from funds we won't receive. In other words, we must receive and accept Jesus as our salvation from sin in order to experience the forgiveness described. By analogy, if someone wants a fresh start and have all their credit card debts forgiven, don't they need to make a petition to the bankruptcy court first? Do they have a valid complaint if they're still in debt next year because they never filed the petition for bankruptcy protection or never asked the court to legally discharge their debts? Do we think the judge is going to just show up at our house some day and say, "Hey, I heard you're in debt trouble? Relax, I've taken care of that and you're now debt free! You're off the hook!" As much as God wants us to experience forgiveness, we must be involved in asking for and accepting this gift.

God is mystery, and the ways that God chooses to act or not act, whether he allows things to happen or prevents them, is also within the realm of mystery. We probably won't be able to understand why God permits terrible disasters or suffering in its various forms. One theory makes some sense. It's better that a person experiences a loss of physical property than the loss of one's soul for all eternity, to be outside the light of heaven and the love of God forever.

Events like a chastisement have the effect of causing an awakening as to what really matters and what is most important. In a similar way, what kind of people would they be if children grew up without ever having been disciplined by their parents? They'd grow up to think they can do whatever they want, whenever they want. The parent knows they have to step in now and then to say, "No, you can't do that." If the child does it again, the parent needs to say more firmly, "No, you can't do that." If the child persists, the parent may next say, "If you do that again, I'll have to punish you." Finally, if they do it again, the parent has to punish them if they can hope or expect the unwanted behavior to change.

It is based on Psalm 86:15 that I wrote previously that God is slow to anger. The Bible also indicates that God is kind, merciful, and forgiving. The mercy of God comes most easily to those who love, are repentant, and are humble. If one is this way, his attitude will go a long way. He or she doesn't have nearly as much to be concerned about as long as his or her repentance is leading them to be a better and more loving person. However, if a person is proud, arrogant, obstinate, unforgiving, or unrepentant and that same person is not willing to change, they are going to run into some very big problems, if they have not already.

"I'm Fine"

I've spoken to a number of people who justify missing Mass/church on weekends with the following belief: "I'm good to others. I love my neighbor. *I'm fine.*" These people are minimizing the significance of their involvement with a church or parish. Love *is* the greatest commandment, but if one truly loves God and one's neighbor, that person will strive to keep the other commandments as well. Jesus said to the apostles gathered at the Last Supper, "If you love me, you will keep my commandments."[127] Sometimes, people get mixed up because they may misinterpret what Christ meant when he said the greatest commandments are to love God and to love one's neighbor (Matthew 22:36-40). Jesus did say this, but some may think this statement nullifies the other commandments. It doesn't. But Jesus did say, "On these two commandments depend the whole Law and the Prophets." Most likely, he clarified this to help people realize what's most important and that it's not about following a rigid sense of do's and don'ts. In other words, what's the point of going to church if somebody's going to be uncharitable afterwards? They missed the most important point which was love. In summation, I really wouldn't disregard any of the commandments, but recognize that love is the most important, both love of God and the love of neighbor. Of the Ten Commandments, I covered the fourth, the fifth, and the seventh in the previous chapter. In the following paragraphs, I'd now like to address the third and the sixth commandments. I write of how Jesus calls us to interpret and apply these now.

A number of people have been deceived into a false notion that kindness to people or charity delivers and excuses them from obeying other instructions of the Lord. It is true that, "love covers a multitude of sins" (1 Peter 4:8, NASB). Love, however, does not give us a license to commit sins. Each transgression still carries its own penalty. Acts of charity work against the penance due us because of such faults. The more generous and loving we are, the more lenient God is to us in relation to our transgressions. When we confess our sins and ask Jesus to forgive us, we're restored to grace, forgiven, and our guilt is removed. This allows us to live in peace. However, a temporal penalty, often called penance, is still due to God in many cases. This is the kind of penalty that loving acts can lessen or mitigate. In short, then, it's not good philosophy to consider oneself free from sin's consequences because of charitable deeds. Loving deeds do lessen such consequences for someone, but there are consequences nonetheless.

Today, people commonly disregard the need to go to church or to live chastely. The sixth commandment is "You shall not commit adultery" (ref. note 120). Skipping church on weekends or sleeping around (with someone to whom we're not married) are *not* behaviors that represent being "good to others." Whether realized or not, these behaviors hurt ourselves, others, and God. One can really abuse himself and others, for example, when engaging in promiscuous sexual activity outside the bond of marriage. Without the solid commitment of marriage, the relationship cannot benefit in the same way from mutual sacrificial love, a love willing to give completely of one's life to the other. Such a commitment helps each person in the marriage to grow as a loving human being. Certainly, people can grow without being married. However, it's my opinion that marriage fosters greater personal growth than cohabitating couples who do not marry. This is because maturity and growth require committed sacrifice in order to overcome the tendency in every person to be self-seeking. For some, this is accomplished through marriage. For others, this is accomplished outside marriage. If one chooses to cohabitate and not marry, they easily circumvent the opportunity for greater personal growth by not committing themselves to their partner in marriage. Though they may say they love each other, how much of this arrangement is a means to use the other person?

On this moral issue, we should also consider the word of God. Consider these words written in a letter from St. Paul: "Do not be deceived; neither fornicators, nor idolaters, nor adulterers, nor boy prostitutes, nor sodomites, nor thieves, nor the greedy, nor drunkards, nor slanderers, nor robbers shall inherit the kingdom of God" (1 Corinthians 6:8-10, NASB). For one engaged in either sex outside marriage or extramarital sex, the concern should be with the words "fornicators" and "adulterers." With the two words combined, most biblical interpretations conclude that the Bible condones only sex within one marriage and that all else is sin.

It's not to condemn anyone for me to believe or write that I consider sex, freely chosen and outside marriage, to be a morally culpable violation of the sixth commandment. God is patient with us, but also expects conversion in this regard. It's important to know the truth for the truth sets us free. I base my opinion concerning sexual morality on the Bible and the teaching of my church. Most Christian denominations interpret the Bible similarly on this matter. Sexual relations have their purposes in God's plan. They are good and meant for good reasons. Otherwise, God would not have created them that way. However, couples need to learn how to make progress with and follow divine wisdom as it pertains to sex and sexuality. A very important dimension of this wisdom in the union of a man and woman is that they each give of themselves in a spirit of loving sacrifice to the other person—not just with the body, but with one's whole life. This union of a man and a woman in marriage is according to God's design. While God had placed Adam in a deep sleep, he took a rib from the side of Adam. From that rib, God fashioned Eve. When he (God) "brought her to the man, the man (Adam) said, "This is now bone of my bones and flesh of my flesh; she shall be called 'Woman,' because she was taken out of Man. For this reason a man shall leave his father and his mother and be joined to his wife; and they shall become one flesh"[128] (Genesis 2:22-24, NASB). Those couples brought together in marriage should also consider the Word of God in this respect. "God created man in His own image, in the image of God He created him; male and female He created them. God blessed them; and God said to them, "Be fruitful and multiply, and fill the earth, and subdue it" (Genesis 1:27-28, NASB).

Morality and Christ

Jesus really challenges us in the area of sexual morality. He expanded the definition of "adultery" and has expected more from his followers than those of the Old Testament. That is because we have the benefit of more grace from his death and resurrection. Thus, it is written, "You have heard that it was said, 'You shall not commit adultery.' But I say to you, everyone who looks at a woman with lust has already committed adultery with her in his heart" (Matthew 5:27-28).[129] The doctrine is understood by the church in a broad sense to mean lust in all its forms. Lusting after *any person*, male or female, is covered by this teaching of Christ. A sexual act is not necessary with another to encroach upon adultery in this context. The mere experience of lusting in one's heart crosses the border into sin. We must discipline the eyes and maintain custody of the eyes. We should also strive to avoid the near occasion of sin and those situations in which we know we're more likely to fall. Don't be discouraged if you find this teaching difficult. God does not expect overnight perfection. What God wants is a willingness to try and a willingness to improve and change. If we should fall, we should make an act of contrition in which we tell God we're sorry and we'll try not to do it again. In the same prayer, we should ask God to forgive us and help us to do better.

Jesus came not to abolish the commandments but to put them in a new perspective and light. We can find this summarized mainly in his Sermon on the Mount (Matthew, chapters 5-7).[130] In this address, Jesus said that not only is it wrong to kill (5th commandment), but that we are liable to judgment even if we *become angry* with our brother.[132] Does that mean we can't get angry? I don't know about you, but I would be in big trouble if that were the case. It has more to do with how we deal with our anger. We should promptly deal with anger before letting it harm a relationship through ill will, bad feelings, gossip, backbiting, slander, violence, etc. Consider the Bible's words: "If you are angry, let it be without sin. The sun must not go down on your wrath; do not give the devil a chance to work on you" (Ephesians 4:26-27).[133]

Mass and Church

A major reason we're supposed to go to Mass or church each week is to express thanksgiving to God for what's been given to us. We also go to make a sacrificial offering of communal worship to the living God. Sometimes, in luxury or excess, some have become lost into thinking that life is more about money and things and some may forget where these things come from. We may not see the good things of our life as God's *blessings*. We should show our thanks by going to *Mass* (or for non-Catholics, by going to a weekly church or worship service). Instead of giving worship and thanksgiving to God, many people have chosen to avoid God and church for whatever reason. People offer many different excuses. The last reason I heard was because a man was still upset at what the church did during *the Inquisition*! Though the injustices done during the Inquisition are validly acknowledged, should abuses from hundreds of years ago keep one out of the house of God now? It is sad that anger keeps many away from church. I encourage people to come back and try church again. Consider forgiveness for the ways certain ministers have failed to adequately communicate God's love or, worse still, have been abusive. Priests and ministers are imperfect and also struggle with sin. While many offer faithful and generous service, others may have hurt you in some way. Please do try to forgive these failings. This is not meant in any way to dismiss anger or anyone's pain. Those difficult feelings exist for good reason. Some people have been hurt, some very badly. We must also remember, however, the words of the Our Father. If we truly understand the meaning of the words Jesus taught in the Our Father, we will only be forgiven our own sins by God *to the extent* that we have been able to *forgive* our brothers and sisters (Matthew 6:9-15).

People have other reasons for missing Mass. Some say they need to shop on Sundays. They say it's the only day during the week they have the time. Others have opted out of Mass because they need to get the kids to soccer or football practice. Still others stayed in because it was too cold or they just didn't feel like going out. Many of these excuses suggest a loss of *faith* from people in society. This can be reversed, but it is important to first understand the problem. It's either priorities are out of order or that people have become so detached from the spiritual that they're not even thinking of going to church services. They may be distracted by things they've got to do. "I pray in my room" is another excuse I've heard about not going to church. God appreciates the prayer, but that person does not comprehend how important their involvement is with their church. What kind of church services would we have if every person said, "I pray in my room" or "I don't believe in organized religion." The priest or minister would be relegated to a private Mass or service. The absence of community worship would have very negative consequences for society. Everyone should think about how to do their part when coming together and how to support their local church.

The third commandment, upheld by Jesus, requires that we "keep holy" the Sabbath day (Exodus 20:8-11). In short, we should make plans to go to a church service every weekend and avoid all unnecessary work on Sundays. Trips to the mall (or even the prayer in the room) are not acceptable excuses to miss church on weekends. Today, many families use kids' soccer practice or games as acceptable excuses to miss weekend services. Those are not good habits to get into and it shows that priorities are out of order. This is teaching kids early on that sports are more important than the worship of God. When I was a teenager, my mom would not let me miss the church service on Sunday. If I was still in bed, she'd get me up before it was too late and drive me there. Sometimes, I had baseball games on Sunday. There was still always a way to get to a church service.

God understands how busy we are. God understands that people don't always feel like going to church. God understands that people may even get bored sometimes with the service. However, God asks that we worship him above all things. So for each person, it's important to reconsider how this should translate into community worship.

Conclusion

This chapter and the previous one are meant to challenge and confront prevailing attitudes in secular media and modern culture that everything is "okay." Everything is far from okay. It's important that we recognize that. We should try to see more clearly along spiritual lines as to why that is the case. Many moral choices have been much more wrong than people have recognized. Some things in society have become messed up as a result. Things don't have to stay that way. We need to listen to the dictates of our conscience and common sense and try to observe the Word of God better in our choices. By all means, let's not derive all our moral education from TV, movies, or the computer. We need to be more attuned to lies contained in secular media about what is acceptable or unacceptable, good or evil, right or wrong. If we let "the world" be our teachers, they will often send false messages. If we live by falsity, we will also live by the consequences of falsity. St. Paul warns of the ill fruit of living by the flesh. "For the one who sows to his own flesh will from the flesh reap corruption, but the one who sows to the Spirit will from the Spirit reap eternal life" (Galatians 6:8, NASB). There is still time to change. Change won't happen overnight, and in some areas of our hearts, change happens very slowly. What can happen quickly is to change our perspective. We can either say "I have no sin" or we can humbly admit "I'm a sinner" and then act accordingly in the sight of God and one another. If our attitude is the former, we cannot be saved. If it is the latter, we can be saved and improve the quality of our lives and soul. With the first attitude, we don't need a savior because the person thinks he or she is all set and will try to be independent. Only the latter can be saved because only this person will turn to Jesus to save his or her soul from the wounded condition by which we're affected.

This chapter and the previous one were written to remind us of the significance of the Word of God, and how the Bible has guided us in the direction of God's good ways. The message of Medjugorje is an echo of the gospel, of the teaching of Christ, and of the Bible. At the same time, some may question the validity of the Medjugorje revelations as being heaven-sent. The Catholic Church itself still tests the various phenomena and the lives of the six visionaries. Thus far, they've not found the content of the Medjugorje messages as being inconsistent with the Bible. However, since the investigation remains ongoing, the next chapter transitions to a summary and outlook on the Church's investigations and statements. This will help one to understand what the Church looks on favorably and what she is still examining and assessing.

> Dear children, do not be of a hard heart towards the mercy of God, which has been pouring out upon you for so much of your time. In this special time of prayer, permit me to transform your hearts that you may help me to have my Son resurrect in all hearts, and that my heart may triumph. (Message of the Virgin Mary to Mirjana Dragićević-Soldo at Medjugorje, April 2, 2007)[134]

Chapter 11

Medjugorje and Church Authority

What does the church have to say about Medjugorje?

I've been asked this reasonable and very good question a number of times. Much has been said by the church, but no final, definitive conclusions have been reached on the issue of whether the reported heavenly messenger is actually believed to be the Mother of God.

The investigation of Medjugorje by the church has been extremely thorough and exhaustive. There have been several different commissions established at different levels of ecclesiastical authority, beginning with the bishop of Mostar's Commission on Medjugorje in the 1980s to the most recent Vatican Commission, established in 2010. I'll comment on the work done and statements made by the various commissions as we proceed in this chapter. I also provide in appendix 3 a number of written statements communicated by Vatican officials and local bishops (of the Medjugorje region), if you should want to investigate the question in more detail from an ecclesiastical point of view.

The Catholic Church has hundreds of years of experience in judging the authenticity of private revelations such as the ones reported at Medjugorje. They follow a very careful and methodical process of evaluation and discernment. This process first tries to rule out every other possible explanation for such a phenomenon, human and otherwise. If they are satisfied they have ruled out everything and that there is no other explanation—other than that it is from God—then it has the chance to be recognized and approved.

Scientific and Psychological Studies Support View That Apparitions Are Authentic

The church relies on the expertise of theologians, scientists, psychiatrists, and psychologists to assist them in establishing the authenticity of apparitions. In terms of ruling everything out on Medjugorje (other than the supernatural), it appears that scientific and theological studies have done just that already (see appendix 2 for full results of scientific, psychological, and theological tests done on visionaries). In their totality, the studies provide evidence the six visionaries have genuinely been seeing someone external and visible only to them. The studies also established that the visionaries have not been lying and that they could not have made up this event. Further, the studies indicated that these reports of apparitions are not caused by hallucinations or psychological illnesses of the visionaries. Theologians further concluded in the tests that this has not been the work of the devil. In supporting these statements, I would point first to the thorough research done by an international French-Italian scientific-theological commission. This was an assembly of seventeen natural scientists, doctors, psychiatrists, and theologians. Together, they came to a twelve-point conclusion on January 14, 1986, in Paina near Milan. As I review their report, it's clear that they ruled out natural interpretations and even the possibility that the visions were being masqueraded by the demonic. They wrote in point no. 4 of their report, "On the basis of information and observations that can be documented, for all and each of the visionaries, it is possible to exclude that these manifestations are of the preternatural order i.e. under demonic influence."[135] Point nos. 1-3 of their conclusions also ruled out (a) fraud and deception, (b) pathological hallucinations, and (c) "a purely natural interpretation of these manifestations."[136] Simply put, one can say that it was not possible for science to explain the experience of the visionaries. Given all of this and the many positive fruits described in the report at Paina, they concluded, "it is well for the Church to recognize the supernatural origin and, thereby, the purpose of the events in Medjugorje."

Other qualified individuals have also asserted strong opinions that Medjugorje is not the work of the devil. In his book, *Is the Virgin Mary Appearing at Medjugorje?* the renowned French Mariologist Father Rene Laurentin refers to the work of Father Robert Faricy, SJ: "Fr. Robert Faricy, SJ, (then) Professor of the Pontifical Gregorian University in Rome, summed up his conclusions in a basic article published in Feu et Lumiere. After having prudently accentuated the fact that, 'the Church has not yet pronounced itself,' his careful examination excludes any simulation or other activity on the part of the devil." [137] He (Father Faricy) "praises 'the healthy doctrine, the human and spiritual qualities of the six young people, and the very positive fruits which constitute the best argument for considering the apparitions as authentic.'" [138]

Father Laurentin continues further in the same book to collect similar judgments on the part of other experts on the spiritual life. He specifically cites as support (assignments or titles may have changed since Laurentin's book was first published):

- The late Cardinal Hans Urs von Balthasar, theologian and spiritual author of the highest quality, who was very interested in Medjugorje. He spoke about it in Rome and helped those responsible for the parish make a responsible evaluation of the present and the future.

- Father Michael Scanlon, President of the University of Steubenville, Ohio;

- Father John Bertolucci of the same university

- Father Beck of Milan, born at Zagreb, director of a retreat house in Milan. He has visited Medjugorje three times

- Father Thomas Forrest, who spent two days at Medjugorje

- Father Tomislav Ivancic, professor of fundamental theology at Zagreb, who also spent two days at Medjugorje

- Father A. Dongo, Belgian theologian

- Father Radogost Grafenauer, SJ, consulted by the bishop of Mostar because of his prudent and critical outlook, has become strongly in favor of the apparitions.

"All these in different degrees exclude a purely natural explanation and, even more, a diabolical influence." [139]

Bishops and Church Authority on Medjugorje

Of the bishops who have spoken with authority on questions regarding Medjugorje, I'd like to first consider opinions expressed by Pope John Paul II. Early on in his papacy, he said, "Medjugorje is the fulfillment and continuation of Fatima."[140] For those not aware, Fatima is an apparition site in Portugal. This was approved by the Catholic Church based on reported visions of the Virgin Mary there in 1917.

Given the positive assessments that have been described of both the visionaries and the Medjugorje event in general, one may wonder why the apparitions haven't already been approved. In general, the church's bishops have been reluctant to communicate a final judgment on the private revelations until the phenomena have ceased and reports of visions have ended. This has not happened over the course of thirty-one years Mary is reported to have been appearing there. The local bishops who investigated this for many years would probably have preferred a major physical and miraculous sign to confirm the supernatural origin. According to the visionaries, one such sign has been promised by the Blessed Virgin on the hill called Podbrdo in Medjugorje. However, this physical miracle has not yet taken place.

Pope John Paul II said to Bishop Hnilica, who served as the Holy Father's advisor for the countries of the East, "Today the world has lost the supernatural. Many people sought it and found it in Medjugorje through prayer, fasting, and through confession" (August 1, 1989 ref. note #140). John Paul II also gave positive assessments to other bishops and priests about the work he saw that the Virgin Mary was doing at Medjugorje. To Bishop Maurillo Kreiger (Brazil), he said in February 1990, "Medjugorje, Medjugorje, it's the spiritual heart of the world."[141] To Bishop Angelo Kim (Korea), he responded to a statement made by Kim that John Paul II had liberated Poland from Communism. The Holy Father replied, "No, this is not my merit. This is the work of the Blessed Virgin Mary as she had predicted in Fatima and in Medjugorje."[142] Archbishop Felipe Santiago Bentez (Paraguay) was seeking the Holy Father's permission to allow Father Slavko Barbaric, a Medjugorje-based Franciscan priest, to go on a speaking tour in his (Ascunsion) Paraguay diocese. Bentez spoke with the pope and said this was his reply: "Authorize everything that concerns Medjugorje."[143] I have confirmed these quotes of Pope John Paul II by reference to two independent sources. For further details, please make reference to the endnotes cited with these quotes.

Rome Confronts the Bishop of Mostar on Medjugorje

The statements of John Paul II were very different and far more positive than those made by the local ranks of the Mostar diocese where Medjugorje is located. In his statements, the pope expressed his faith and belief that the Virgin Mary was at work in Medjugorje.

He was well aware that voices like Bishop Žanić, then bishop of the Mostar diocese, were saying either "This has not been approved" or "We view these apparitions in the negative."

"Entrusted by Rome with the Commission of Inquiry as local bishop, he (Bishop Žanić) submitted a negative judgment (on Medjugorje) to (then) Cardinal Ratzinger in 1986."[144]

At that time, Ratzinger (now Pope Benedict XVI) was serving under John Paul II as head of the Congregation for the Doctrine of the Faith at the Vatican. According to numerous sources, Cardinal Ratzinger took authority away from Bishop Žanić on the Medjugorje question after Žanić submitted his negative report. Ordinarily, the church gives authority on judging apparitions solely to the *local bishop* of the locality where the visions are reported. For Medjugorje, that's the bishop of the Mostar diocese. In 1987, however, Rome decided to give authority on Medjugorje to the wider delegation of the Yugoslavian Bishops' Conference.

"But Cardinal Ratzinger rejected these negative conclusions. And—an event without precedent in the history of apparitions—the local bishop (Msgr. Žanić) was relieved of the dossier. Rome dissolved Bishop Žanić's Commission and then put the matter in the hands of the Yugoslavian Episcopal Conference. A new commission was consequently appointed under the presidency of Bishop Komarica (of Banja Luka, Bosnia-Herzegovina)."[145]

Yugoslavia split up into different countries following their civil war from 1991-1995, so the Yugoslavian Bishops' Conference was likewise dissolved during this period. Authority on the Medjugorje question then went to the bishops of the newly established country of Bosnia and Herzegovina. This new commission of bishops was formed in 1995.

Vatican Takes Over Work of Investigation in 2010

A very significant shift concerning investigation of the Medjugorje phenomena took place in 2010. Previously, Rome entrusted the work of investigation to the local bishops of the diocese and then of the country where Medjugorje is located. Rome has now taken over the work of investigation and evaluation of Medjugorje. In March 2010, Pope Benedict XVI appointed Cardinal Camilio Ruini, an Italian cardinal, to head a new commission to report to the Congregation of the Doctrine of the Faith to investigate these events. The established International Commission is made up of cardinals, bishops, and experts concerning the study of apparitions. "Fr. Federico Lombardi, Director of Holy See Press Office, explained that the mentioned Commission will be operating with full discretion, and that all results that will follow after a long term operation will be delivered to (the) Congregation for the Doctrine of the Faith. Archbishop Allessandro D'Errico, Apostolic Nuncio to Bosnia and Herzegovina, gave this information to bishops of the Bishop's Conference of Bosnia and Herzegovina, as instructed by Cardinal Secretary of State, Tarcisio Bertone."[146]

The new International Commission on Medjugorje has begun its complex work of investigation, and we don't know when exactly they will come forth with an official pronouncement. However, it's been reported that they will communicate their findings to the Vatican before the end of 2012. However, a Bosnian news agency called Oslobodjenje recently issued a report which said the commission's work will continue into 2013. Medjugorjetoday.tv claims to have information running contrary to this story. They indicated in an article on their website August 31, 2012 that the Commission was in the final stages of preparing its report to the Vatican, "if the report has not already been sent." Either way, we will soon know which account is correct.

Medjugorje and Official Statements of Church Authority

In the meantime, it's important to address the extensive work that has already been done by the bishops of the region where Medjugorje is located. It's they, as a body, to whom the Catholic Church entrusted authority on the Medjugorje issues through the year 2010. So it's important to illustrate what they said in their official capacity. If you're looking for a statement that says, "We believe the apparitions at Medjugorje are supernatural" or "We believe the reported apparitions at Medjugorje are not supernatural," this section may disappoint you. The local bishops didn't reach a conclusion, "We believe this is (or is not) the Virgin Mary." They chose to *leave open* this question in order to continue following the event as it unfolds in the lives of the six visionaries. Upon meeting in Croatia in 1991, the local bishops issued their official statement on Medjugorje, called the Declaration at Zadar (printed below). The Declaration at Zadar remains the church's position on Medjugorje until another authoritative position is declared.

Declaration of the Ex-Yugoslavia Bishops' Conference on Medjugorje

At the ordinary session of the Bishops' Conference of Yugoslavia in Zadar from April 9-11, 1991, the following was adopted:

DECLARATION

The bishops, from the very beginning, have been following the events of Medjugorje through the Bishop of the diocese (Mostar), the Bishop's Commission and the Commission of the Bishops Conference of Yugoslavia on Medjugorje.

On the basis of the investigations, so far it cannot be affirmed that one is dealing with supernatural apparitions and revelations.

However, the numerous gatherings of the faithful from different parts of the world, who come to Medjugorje, prompted both by motives of belief and various other motives, require the attention and pastoral care in the first place of the diocesan bishop and with him of the other bishops also, so that in Medjugorje and in everything connected with it a healthy devotion to the Blessed Virgin Mary may be promoted in accordance with the teaching of the Church.

For this purpose, the bishops will issue especially suitable liturgical-pastoral directives. Likewise, through their Commission they will continue to keep up with and investigate the entire event in Medjugorje.

In Zadar April 10, 1991
The Bishops of Yugoslavia [147]

Commentary on the Declaration at Zadar

When I first read the bishops' official statement, I didn't really like it that much. It could easily have been misconstrued to indicate that a healthy devotion to the Virgin Mary did not already exist or that such had not already been soundly promoted. Clearly, these realities already existed at the time this statement was issued in 1991. The existing positive fruits of Medjugorje were subsequently recognized by the bishops of that region. However, while these positive assessments have been stated by such church officials, they are not yet incorporated into the Church's official "Zadar Declaration."

The bishops of Yugoslavia issued the declaration after a thorough review of what took place in Medjugorje and extensive examination of the six visionaries. By using language like "so far" and adding that they will continue to "keep up with" and "investigate the entire

Malloy

---

event," they communicated that the question has not reached the point of a final declaration. (Then) Cardinal Ratzinger clarified this: "In September 1991, during a conference in Vienna, Cardinal Ratzinger declared that no definitive position had been taken by the church as yet. 'We are open. The commission proceeds with its work. One must continue to wait and pray.'" [148]

Shortly after the Zadar pronouncement, Yugoslavia entered into a disastrous civil war. On June 26, 1991, Serbia attacked Slovenia and the civil war had begun. The developing carnage became widely known as a humanitarian nightmare caused by a pattern of "ethnic cleansing" practices of warring factions. Muslims, Croats, and Serbs of the different Yugoslavian provinces had many interlocking battles for four years as province after province declared independence from the long-existing Communist rule of the original country. During that summer of 1991, Mary was reportedly trying to convince people of the gravity of the problem they were facing:

> Dear children! At this time peace is being threatened in a special way, and I am seeking from you to renew fasting and prayer in your families. I desire you to grasp the seriousness of the situation and that much of what will happen depends on your prayers and you are praying a little bit. Dear children, I am with you and I am inviting you to begin to pray and to fast seriously as in the first days of my coming. Thank you for having responded to my call (July 25, 1991) . . . I call you dear children to now grasp the importance of my coming and the seriousness of the situation . . . (August 25, 1991)[149]

Commentary from Bishop Ratko Perić, Bishop of Mostar

Bishop Ratko Perić was appointed the bishop of Mostar on July 24, 1993, following the retirement of Bishop Pavao Žanić. Overall, this still-current bishop has been negative concerning the heavenly identity of Medjugorje's frequent apparition visitor. Rome has clarified, however, that though he is entitled to express such opinion as the local bishop, the Vatican views it as just that, his opinion.

Bishop Perić did make some more positive comments, however, when confirming 150 children in Medjugorje in 1993. In his homily, he summarized important points made by the bishops who investigated Medjugorje, namely:

1.) Medjugorje is officially accepted as a place of prayer and worship

2.) A liturgical and pastoral team is responsible for ensuring the rightful status of the Virgin in the offices of the Parish

3.) The (Bishops') Commission has declared a *"non constat de supernaturalitate"* (the Latin phrase signifies that at the present stage of investigation, it is *not yet* possible to declare the supernatural reality of the phenomena, but that such a possibility *remains open* for the future).[150]

Clarification Made on Zadar Declaration by Cardinal Kuharic

Cardinal Franjo Kuharic, while serving as archbishop of Zagreb (Croatia) and as president of the Bishops' Conference on Medjugorje, made this clarifying statement on the Declaration at Zadar in an interview with the newspaper *Glas Koncila,* August 15, 1993:

> After three years of study conducted by the appropriate Commission, we bishops have accepted Medjugorje as a holy place, as a shrine. This means that we have nothing against it if someone venerates the Mother of God in a manner also in agreement with the teaching and belief of the Church . . . This is why we leave this question

to further studies of the Church. The Church does not hurry.[151]

Cardinal Kuharic's statement shows that the bishops respectfully acknowledge the holiness of the village and the spiritual fruits present there. They've accepted it as a holy place. It's even identified by Cardinal Kuharic as a shrine. Medjugorje is recognized as a place of prayer where one is free to go on pilgrimage if one chooses. At the same time, the statement expresses a cautious "wait and see" approach, which has been characteristic of the investigations.

Bishop Žanić and Church Politics on Medjugorje

The former bishop of Mostar, Bishop Pavao Žanić, flip-flopped his position concerning the Medjugorje situation. He was initially favorable toward the Medjugorje visionaries during the summer of 1981, shortly after learning of the initial reports of apparitions. However, he later became one of the visionaries' and Medjugorje's strongest adversaries. The negative stance he took on the apparitions set up early roadblocks to those who otherwise wished to propagate the good, which was so often Medjugorje's effect. Bishop Žanić came out in support of the six visionaries during the summer of 1981. He gave a positive statement that said the visionaries were "not lying." Consider, however, some events that took place subsequent to such support. These events may help to explain why he went from friend to foe on the support of Medjugorje.

Communists Probably Threatened Bishop Žanić

Bishop Žanić probably became fearful of the reaction of the (then-Communist) government about his initially favorable statements about the Gospa at Medjugorje. He didn't want to go to jail because of this matter. Some pretty good evidence exists that he was threatened in 1981 by the Yugoslavian Communist government after making initially favorable comments concerning the visionaries. At that time, the government viewed the popular Medjugorje event as somewhat of a political insurgency or plot against the government. The pastor of Medjugorje's St. James Parish (Father Jozo Zovko) was sent to jail by the government for his support of the visionaries and support of the Gospa's message: "On August 17, 1981, Fr. Jozo was arrested and, in the end, sentenced to 3 ½ years of hard labor because of his stand on Medjugorje."[152] It's no secret or question that Father Jozo actually did jail time. It's a fact of history, and a movie was even created about his trial and imprisonment called *Gospa* (1995), starring Martin Sheen. Apparently, Bishop Žanić didn't feel like confronting the same fate. When confronted with a choice between his continued support of Medjugorje and jail/punishment by the government, I'll conclude he chose to give up the former to avoid the latter. I quote Dr. Ljudevit Rupčić as support. According to his book *The Truth About Medjugorje*, Father Jozo (Zovko) was released from prison on February 18, 1983. "Immediately after he was released from prison, February 18, 1983, Fr. Jozo paid a visit to the bishop."[153] The 1983 dialogue between Father Jozo and Bishop Žanić, as recorded by Dr. Rupčić, indicates that Bishop Žanić tried to avoid going to prison over Medjugorje: "The bishop tried on this occasion to justify his actions, stating that . . . it was not 'possible' for him to have acted differently than he did, threatened as he was by the UDBA (State Security) with imprisonment. Besides this, he mentioned once again the pressure brought to bear on him from diocesan priests . . . not to intervene on Medjugorje's behalf. He said that priests had written, reproaching him for his support of the apparitions. These (diocesan) priests were against Medjugorje and feared that the Franciscans would gain prestige if the apparitions were approved."[154]

It sounds like the bishop was under much pressure to change his position about the situation in Medjugorje and the visionaries. He probably gave into pressure from the government and even his own priests to go from speaking in favor of Medjugorje to going silent on it and then, ultimately, to working against it. It also appears as if some Mostar-area diocesan priests had a relationship problem toward Franciscan priests. It sounds like they did not like the notoriety that Franciscan priests like Father Jozo Zovko were receiving from the public because of the popularity of Medjugorje or popularity with the parishioners in general.

The Case of Father Vego

Consider also Bishop Žanić's outlook on the case of Father Ivaca Vego. Father Vego was a Franciscan priest within Bishop's Žanić's diocese who was suspended from the priesthood and then expelled from the Franciscan order. Bishop Žanić supported the case for his removal on the grounds of disobedience. According to the visionary Vicka's diary, the Virgin Mary revealed to the visionaries that Father Vego was "not guilty."[155]

I am not aware of reasons that the Virgin Mary cited for Father Vego's innocence. However, Dr. Rupčić writes in *The Truth about Medjugorje:* "Vego was punished not only without proper judicial procedure and against canon law, but without a hearing, before being expelled from the Order . . . even his right of appeal was denied. Experts in canon law are unanimous in asserting that, without due process and proper juridical procedures, Vego's punishment is null and void."[156] The obvious problem was that Father Vego had already been expelled from the Franciscans. Dr. Rupčić sheds some light on this new difficulty for the bishop: "The question here (and the Gospa's remarks) refers only to the bishop's canonical procedures and the punishments meted out to Vego, nothing else. That Vego desired to find out through the visionaries what the (Virgin Mary) thought about (his) dilemma is, to a certain degree, understandable. And, to this inquiry, the "Gospa," according to the visionaries, responded that they were *not guilty*." [157] (A Father Prusina was also referred to in this quote, explaining the word "they").

Bishop Žanić was reportedly very much displeased to learn of the various entries from Vicka's diary concerning Our Lady's reported reaction to Fathers Vego and Prusina. Bishop Žanić had concluded previously that Father Vego was guilty and thereby prohibited him from exercising the priesthood. Bishop Žanić probably became upset and fearful to learn that the Gospa implied he was wrong.

Blessed Are Those Who Have Not Seen and Believed

Aside from the political environment, God still leaves room for faith in the Medjugorje event and miracle. God calls for faith from all, including those priests and bishops who investigate the phenomena. As we read the message of Medjugorje or the words of Christ himself in the Gospels, how much are we called to faith and how much are we called to evidence? They've called us to faith, to be a believing people. We don't have to duplicate the sophistication of *CSI Miami* in investigating the apparitions. Yes, we must be prudent and cautious with such an event, especially one that forecasts future chastisement and has called people to a higher-than-normal standard in living the spiritual life. And our faith should be reasonable. We must test the various prophecies and those proclaiming them. To confirm Mary's identity and many messages, there must be solid reasons for believing it and we should not act instead on a blind or overzealous faith.

Empowered by the Spirit, it's my opinion that Mary has been accomplishing what she set out to do, as explained during the first week of the visions: "I wish to be with you to convert and to reconcile the whole world" (June 26, 1981, ref. note #75). Since then, people from all parts of the world have given witness to the particular role of the Medjugorje event in their relationship with Christ, the Virgin, and their conversion. Do we not already have a "miracle" the world over?

We should recognize the works of God and be able to discern the wisdom, words, and heart of Mary. If one needs evidence, reasonable evidence already exists. Other evidence, for example, is in the young people she led to seminary, priesthood, or consecrated religious life. For example, I know three priests in my diocese who made pilgrimages to Medjugorje before they even applied to St. John's Seminary in Boston. I know a fourth, a Franciscan, who had not gone on pilgrimage to Medjugorje but was ordained also. Before he entered the seminary, his conversion began by reading a book on the message of Our Lady of Medjugorje. There are others who went to seminary or novitiate or came forward for ordination because of the work of God through Our Lady of Medjugorje. Father Danko Perutina, a Franciscan priest, confirmed my belief concerning these vocations. Father Danko is on staff at the Medjugorje parish, St. James Church, and has been collecting testimonials from people who have reported vocations directly as a result of their Medjugorje experiences. Father Danko reported that, thus far, the parish had collected over one thousand credible written accounts of individuals who reported their vocations came through Medjugorje. As I understand it, this study is still a work in process, but should be very influential as the church continues to evaluate Medjugorje's good fruits.

Medjugorje Has Positive Impact on the World's Youth

This may sound like an extraordinary assessment, but there are most likely millions of youth by now who have experienced the grace of God through the Medjugorje event. Already in 1983, Cardinal Franjo Kuharic (Croatia) told his friend Rev. David du Plessis, "How can I doubt that Medjugorje is God's doing? . . . Do you know that half a million young people have surrendered to Christ? The Lord is stirring this country. They need fifty to sixty priests every weekend, just to hear confessions and to counsel these young people!"[158] I was in Medjugorje during August 2010 for the annual youth festival there. I've never seen so many young people gathered for worship at Mass—and really enjoying it at that. The music and liturgy were outstanding, and I was amazed at how much the young people were responding and engaged in these experiences each night. It was truly encouraging. There was an estimated forty-five thousand youth gathered in Medjugorje that week for this annual youth festival (called Mladifest), which is celebrated each year the first week of August. Again in 2012, the Youth Festival drew an estimated forty thousand young people representing some seventy nations.

Conclusion

Anyone will be able to believe in Medjugorje once the physical miracle comes, once the Great Sign is left on the hill. In the meantime, the bishop of Mostar, Ratko Perić, has stated publicly that he does not believe in the supernatural character of the apparitions. If he's still with us, he will not be able to deny the truth when the full evidence comes. While some wait and require more evidence, are they being more like Thomas? Thomas said to the other apostles regarding reports of Jesus's resurrection from the dead, "Unless I see the mark of the nails in his hands and put my finger into the nail marks and put my hand into his side, I will not believe."[159] The risen Jesus appeared on the scene one week later to be with Thomas and the other apostles. He said to Thomas, "Put your finger here and see my hands, and bring your hand and put it into my side, and do not be unbelieving, but believe." Thomas responded by saying, "My Lord and my God!" Jesus said to him, "Have you come to believe because you have seen me? Blessed are those who have not seen and have believed."[160]

> Dear children! Also today I call you to conversion. May your life, little children, be a reflection of God's goodness and not of hatred and unfaithfulness. Pray, little children, that prayer may become life for you. In this way, in your life you will discover the peace and joy

which God gives to those who have an open heart to His love. And you, who are far from God's mercy, convert so that God may not become deaf to your prayers and that it may not be too late for you. Therefore, in this time of grace, convert and put God in the first place in your life. Thank you for having responded to my call. (Our Lady of Medjugorje's "Monthly Message to the World," given through Maria Pavlović-Lunetti, August 25, 2007)[161]

Chapter 12

Road to Peace

I'm near completion of this project. It's the final chapter, but I know that the story is far from finished. It will be a divine hand that will write the final chapters of this lengthy supernatural drama. From his own hand and from the font of God's mercy, we will continue to experience this extraordinary intervention at Medjugorje. By his own providence, it's my opinion that God will also manifest certain major events to occur on earth, to be prophesied by the visionaries beforehand. These happenings, including the promised physical sign on Podbrdo, will confirm the authenticity of the Virgin Mary's apparitions at Medjugorje. For those who will not respond to mercy, time, grace, or warnings, we will also witness manifestations of divine justice as prophesied by the Virgin and communicated by means of secrets to the six seers.

To make some final points in this book, I'm going to make what will probably seem like an unexpected and unusual shift. I'm going to shift from the very high, sublime, and supernatural character of the Medjugorje apparitions to the more common and popular topic of sports. Yes, sports. Why am I doing this? I know there will be some people who I'll be unable to reach on the Medjugorje topic without some comparison to the ever-popular and very well-understood sports world. In addition, there are some analogies by which anyone can compare sports events to our spiritual journey.

Boston, the area where I grew up and still live in, is a *very big* sports town. If I'm not current on the Boston Bruins, Celtics, Red Sox, and New England Patriots, I lose opportunities to connect with people about all sorts of things. I accept, to a degree, the profound devotion New Englanders have for their beloved sports teams. I've had some of it myself. I have always been a die-hard Red Sox fan since I was a small boy. I remember being very saddened and disappointed following the defeat of the Red Sox by the New York Mets in the 1986 World Series. However, I celebrated with many other Red Sox fans over our play-off comeback against the archrival New York Yankees in 2004. The Sox were down 3-0 against the Yanks in a best of seven-game series. In remarkable fashion, the Sox went on to win the next four games of the series. The defeat of the Yankees paved the way for a sweep of the Cardinals in the 2004 World Series. We also celebrated *another* Red Sox World Series championship in 2007, the second time they did this in three years! Clearly, the eighty-six-year old curse had been broken, a curse many believed to be on the Red Sox club since the last time they won the World Series in 1918.

In football, the New England Patriots were like folk heroes during the previous decade, beginning with their first of three Super Bowl victories in 2002. They went on to win two additional Super Bowl titles in 2004 and 2005, respectively. Despite our disappointing loss to the New York Giants in Super Bowl Forty-Two (2008) and a loss again to the Giants in Super Bowl Forty-Six (2012), the Patriots have still won three of the last eleven Super Bowls. I think Quarterback Tom Brady and the Pats will win at least one more Super Bowl together before Brady's completes his career. The basketball team, the Boston Celtics, has won the NBA championship seventeen times, more than any other team in the NBA. Their most recent title came in 2008 against the Los Angeles Lakers. The hockey team, the Boston Bruins, won the Stanley Cup championship in 2011, the first time the Bruins won the coveted Stanley Cup in thirty-nine years. The Bruins' hard-fought, gritty, and aggressive performance helped them edge out a very talented Vancouver Canucks team.

The Bruins have also been very popular among the Boston fan base, especially now as a recent Stanley Cup champion. And who could forget Doug Flutie's "Hail Mary" pass to Gerard Phelan in the last seconds of a 1984 college football game between Boston College and the Miami Hurricanes? I was watching the game while on Thanksgiving break from school. With BC down 45-41 and six seconds left on the game clock, Flutie threw a remarkable pass from the Eagles' own 37-yard line into the end zone. Wide-receiver Phelan, who had run just ahead of Hurricane defenders, pulled in the pass while falling to the ground and BC won the game 47-45! This was the most exciting college football game I have ever seen.

That's it for my analysis of the Boston sports scene. I've tried to be as concise as I could regarding a heavily strong sports-inundated city. Whether we're speaking of Boston sports fans or many other fans, have you ever noticed just how emotional people get about these athletic contests? It can really get pretty intense. Many sports fans and athletes become ecstatic, depressed, angry, or jubilant depending on whether they or their team play well or poorly, wins or loses. In football, fans get excited over every first down, field goal, sack, and touchdown. They get excited when we recover the ball from the other side through fumbles and interceptions. We groan if our quarterback should throw an interception or if one of our linemen is caught "offside" or found guilty of "holding." We have all this love and devotion to our special team, and that's okay. In the back of my mind though, I'm wondering about this question. *Can we get this excited about God?* So many people get excited about *sports*. Can we also develop this much enthusiasm about our Maker?

Why do so many people celebrate the World Series or the Super Bowl more than they celebrate the person of Jesus Christ? Why would five thousand people travel across the country from Boston to go to a Patriots' play-off game, but they can't go to Sunday Mass, a three-minute drive down the street? Why will other people pay $2,000 to see the Red Sox or Patriots in the play-offs, but they can't give more than a dollar or two to the collection basket?

Mary did not come to Medjugorje to spoil the excitement of sports or anything else that is good, clean fun. Sports are good and they are of God. However, one's devotion to sports can be overdone. The Mother of God reminds us often to consider God, salvation, our soul, prayer, and worship. She asks us to really choose the Lord Jesus Christ as the one and only God in our life. Mary is commissioned and sent by God on a special mission at Medjugorje to direct humankind to its salvation and peace in Christ. As Queen of Heaven and Earth, she's been given a role as the messenger of God's peace plan in Christ for humanity. Many human souls are at stake in times that she describes as urgent. With a gentle yet firm motherly love for every human on earth, she's leading as many as possible to peace and to heaven. In my opinion, she's been active in this Medjugorje project for thirty-one years. That should tell us that something is definitely up.

Hopefully, it's not our time yet. All of us are called to conversion, and we have time to change as I write this now. However, the sand on the hourglass won't run forever! We're being called to focus on higher things. We are called to raise our minds and hearts toward heaven. We're being asked to turn the TV off now, put the clicker aside, and tune into God. With the TV, can we at least watch a Christian or Catholic cable broadcast as part of our scheduling? The point is that we need to go beyond the Red Sox, *Law & Order*, and *CNN*.

If you haven't already, try to incorporate into your life each week the messages of the Virgin Mary. In her message is the same call of the Gospel but with a special focus on conversion, prayer, penance, and faith for the times in which we live. You may prefer to use the Bible as a daily meditation. Meditation on a passage of the Bible is an excellent way to start praying. The rosary (see appendix 4) is another excellent way to start praying. Many times, I get started with five decades of the rosary. By the time I'm finished with the rosary, I've been able to detach enough from worldly distractions to be able to focus on God. To get prayer started, do whatever works best for you to get in touch with God. Get as relaxed as possible and try to meditate. Don't let anybody infringe on your prayer time and don't get discouraged if it doesn't seem like anything happens right away. Make appointments and commitments with God that nobody can break. The visionary Ivan says that if we can be so good about making appointments to watch our favorite TV programs, we should be just as effective at keeping our appointments with God.

Is God Our Lord?

We can know who the God is in our life by considering what we care about the most. In the sports examples cited previously, it happens all the time that a person will devote himself more to a team or a human person than the Lord. Why is it so? Why will a person not visit God in church, but will go cross-country to see a sports team on the opposite coast? *Now* is the best time to address these issues—not in our eighties or when we're dead and buried. For many people, they don't want to confront the spiritual issues and come into close contact with God. Many are afraid to address the deeper issues of their soul. Others are angry at God for something that happened or did not happen. We must talk to God about these things and communicate. If we're angry at God, we must tell him that and why. God waits for our hearts to open back up to him, but at some point we must decide for him. Disconnected from that life source, our spirits would eventually grow cold and deteriorate.

I'm reminded of an old commercial for the Fram oil filter. The mechanic says to the car owner, "You can pay me now . . . or pay me later." In other words, if he pays money for the oil filter now and has it installed, he can avoid paying much larger sums later on for engine repairs. Our spiritual can be analogous. If we don't address the spiritual issues now, we'll need to do so later. Why put it off and let these matters accumulate? As Boston priest Father Tom DiLorenzo says, encouraging Catholics to go to confession, "Go now . . . and avoid the rush!" If you're not Catholic and don't go to confession, one must still address the significant matters of his or her soul. Why put off Jesus, church, our prayer, our salvation? These are *the most important things.*

The Reality of Purgatory and Hell

It is difficult to consider places a soul could go after this life other than heaven. As someone who believes in hell's existence and that many souls have gone there, what kind of a priest would I be if I did not confirm for readers that hell is possible for some, even many? For those who choose to reject God, the cost is eternal if this choice goes without repentance. Mirjana pleads with us to pray for unbelievers every day. Unbelievers can certainly refer to atheists, but in a broader sense it is those who have not yet come to know the love of God. They are in serious need of prayer and their fate is grim if they persist in unbelief despite all the ways that God tries to show them that he's real. Mirjana has been shown the fate of unbelievers and she said it has caused her much suffering. She said that the Virgin has asked all of us to pray for them.

I do not believe that God condemns any person to hell. My understanding is that those who go to hell, in effect, choose it for themselves. That is because they choose to reject God right up to their moment of judgment. If you do not believe in hell, consider reading from the Bible the passage in Matthew 25:41-46. Based on these words of Christ and other biblical revelations such as 2 Thessalonians 1:8-9, the Catholic Church and most Christian denominations believe that, not only does hell exist, but that it is permanent for those who go there. There is no turning back after one enters hell. Why is this so? God is eternal and our souls are created for eternity. As such, the choice to accept or reject God is an eternal choice. So if a person obstinately chooses to reject God and refuses to accept the salvation God offers, his eternal destination becomes hell after he has been judged. Mary teaches at Medjugorje that if a person goes to hell, the person has chosen hell as his destination. Sadly, this person has come to the point where he wants nothing to do with God. Thus, he cannot accept the salvation that God wants to give him. Read appendix 1 to confirm more how this is so. This includes an interview with the visionaries Jakov and Vicka, who were both taken to heaven, hell, and purgatory by Our Lady of Medjugorje. They confirmed through their private revelations the existence of hell, as well as heaven and purgatory.

Purgatory is a middle ground, if you will. People who go to purgatory have accepted and chosen for Christ, and by grace, are thereby saved for eternity. However, their souls are not ready for heaven, so they go to this place for further purification. Souls do suffer in purgatory according to the private revelations at Medjugorje. We also learn through Medjugorje that there are levels in purgatory, with each level being closer to heaven. The lower the level of a soul in purgatory, the greater the suffering that takes place for him there. As he or she comes higher, the suffering becomes less. It's a very good thing to pray for all the souls in purgatory and to remember all of our loved ones who have died.

"The Catholic Church gives the name *Purgatory* to this final purification of the elect, which is entirely different from the punishment of the damned. The Church formulated her doctrine of faith on Purgatory especially at the Councils of Florence and Trent. The tradition of the Church, by reference to certain texts of scripture, speaks of a cleansing fire (1 Corinthians 3:15; 1 Peter 1:7):

> As for certain lesser faults, we must believe that, before the Final Judgment, there is a purifying fire. He who is truth says that whoever utters blasphemy against the Holy Spirit will be pardoned neither in this age nor in the age to come (Matthew 12:32). From this sentence we understand that certain offenses can be forgiven in this age, but certain others in the age to come" (from the English Translation of the *Catechism of the*

Catholic Church, copyright 1994, United States Catholic Conference, Inc.), section 1031.

Ultimately and essentially, our options are heaven or hell and this choice is ours to make. We're saved by God's grace in Christ and we cannot be saved without grace. If we accept God, we won't go to hell. We'll go to heaven if we're ready; otherwise, we go to purgatory until we're ready to go to heaven. My theological understanding is that we must accept and believe in Jesus Christ to be saved and enter eternal life in heaven. There is no one on this earth we should judge who is beyond salvation. That judgment is God's alone to make. God desires every one of us to be saved, without exception.

Medjugorje is not about chastisement, purgatory, or hell, but is about a mother in heaven who loves us and is guiding us on a pathway to peace and to paradise. We're being guided through many words of wisdom. Mary's intercession before God is designed to bring us into a close relationship with Jesus Christ whom she identifies as our salvation. In response to a question about oriental meditations such as Zen and Transcendentalism, Our Lady said at Medjugorje, "Why do you call them 'meditations,' when it deals with human works? The true meditation is a meeting with Jesus. When you discover joy, interior peace, you must know there is only one God, and only one Mediator, Jesus Christ"[162] (December 25, 1984).

Conversion and Sports

If you're on the wrong path, Mary is clear at Medjugorje: *do not delay your conversion.* Conversion of the heart and soul take much time. Allow me, if you will, to allude back to the sports scene in this section. I want to go back to this because these last paragraphs have included some heavy and difficult material and it is better to revert now to something less intense. Remember my discussion of the Patriots earlier in the chapter? Would they have won those three Super Bowls if Coach Bill Belichick and his staff did not go over the game plan and prepare the offense and defense for battle against the opposing sides? Would they have won the Super Bowls if quarterback Tom Brady just hung out with Bill Belichick and the other members of the team, played cards, and watched reruns of Super Bowl XX against the Chicago Bears? Of course they wouldn't. They had to go to work and get ready to do battle with their opponent. What if Doug Flutie and the rest of the B.C. Eagles just casually approached their last drive during that game in Miami? It's very unlikely that they would have achieved the same results.

The same is true in the spiritual life. We have our own opponents in life, and we must battle too, to do well and avoid the bad. This is not a time to procrastinate when it comes to the things of God. It's not a time to be indifferent to spiritual things or to dismiss the reality of sin. If we haven't already, we need to *begin* the work of prayer and conversion. Otherwise, our weaknesses will catch up with us, and all of a sudden, we'll find ourselves outscored 49-0 with two minutes left on the clock. Yes, we've lost this match, but we have another chance with God. God has a *new way*, but we won't experience the success of it unless we let go of our old ways. Let's not use a 1985 game plan for a 2012 reality. The Patriots wouldn't have fared very well if they used the same game plan against the Philadelphia Eagles in Super Bowl Thirty-Nine as they used in Super Bowl Thirty-Six against the St. Louis Rams. The plan for Super Bowl Thirty-Six was relevant for 2002, but it wasn't 2002 anymore. They were playing a different team and it was three years later. So they went to work again, developed a new plan, followed through on the field, and they won again. We'll win too—in life and the afterlife—if we have a spiritual life and keep God number one, above all persons and things. We'll win too if we keep God number one even when our faith is tested and we hit the bumps in the road associated with the cross. We'll win too if we're willing to do things differently, amending our lives in accordance with God's will and plans. And if things still look bleak or you get discouraged or things just aren't working out your way, don't give up. Sometimes, you'll end up winning simply because you hung in there and didn't quit. Take a chance if you need to, throw a Hail Mary pass, but do everything you can in order not to quit.

We probably don't have a great deal of time to change and choose for God in our life. The urgency was reflected in Mary's words given through Marija on August 25, 2007: "And you, who are far from God's mercy, convert so that God may not become deaf to your prayers and that it may not be too late for you."[163]

Understanding True Devotion to Mary

A spiritual relationship with the Madonna helps a person greatly on the path of conversion, for those who trust her and invoke her help. Our fellow Christians from other denominations should understand that Catholics do not worship Mary. The Catholic Church has never taught us to worship her as if she were some form of deity. Some excessively zealous devotees err on the side of worshiping Mary, but if they do so, this is their mistake. This is not the way the church teaches us to relate to the Mother of God. The church teaches us to honor and to be devoted to the Virgin Mary, to venerate her. This devotion is due Mary, the church believes, because of her special and unique relationship to Jesus Christ as his mother and as faithful disciple who stood before him while he was dying on the cross. The devotion we offer Mary is not worship, and it is far different from the worship we offer to Jesus Christ.

A believer can, of course, go directly to Jesus, who says, "Come to me all, you who labor and are burdened, and I will give you rest."[164] I don't know of anywhere in the Bible where it says that we cannot go directly to Christ. If one reads the various biblical accounts when people went to Jesus and asked him for help, I can't recall him turning away anyone. He would test their faith, but always welcomed those who approached him humbly. The mother of Christ offers a most effective and humble means by which to draw closer to her Son.

Jesus is our salvation and our peace. Mary can work toward our salvation and obtain graces from God which assist us in that regard and with our spiritual life in general. She invites us to a relationship with her as a spiritual mother. Within that relationship, she directs us to her Son. Authentic Marian devotion, properly understood and practiced, cannot take anything away from our relationship with Christ. It can only add something positive to it. United with Mary and her intercession with grace, we're more easily able to discover this place close to the heart of her Son.

Surrendering and "Letting Go"

I don't like surrender and I've found it very difficult. But we must *let go and let God,* as the saying goes. We have a choice: choose God's way or against God's way. Mary desperately pleads at Medjugorje to surrender to God and choose God's ways. She has used the word "surrender" much and indicates that our full measure of peace is dependent on such surrender to God: "I beseech you, surrender to the Lord your entire past" (February 25, 1987).[165]

Yes, let go of the past. It's all over and we can't change a thing about it now. Let's not permit the devil to "reaccuse" us for mistakes or sins that we've already repented of and been forgiven. He would be happy to keep us on that guilt trip. If we haven't repented yet and confessed, let's go ahead and do that now. Let's take our sins to the cross and repent because Jesus wants us to be free of the guilt and the regrets. That's why he died on a cross. Let's be reconciled with God and get rid of guilt! Christ won the victory over sin and death on Calvary. Let's move on and resurrect with him. He paid the price for our sin debt *in full*!

"I call each one of you to decide to surrender everything completely to me . . ." (Nov. 25, 1987).

"I am calling you to prayer and complete surrender to God . . ." (Feb. 25, 1988).

161

"I am calling you to a complete surrender to God . . ." (March 25, 1988).[166]

Again and again, Mary pleads for complete surrender to God. In my walk, I've been asked to give up self-will and control and turn that over to God, yielding to his will alone. I'm still working on it. It can only be accomplished through prayer and a growing trust in God. I've prayed much, but trusting God has come more slowly. Only in a spiritual journey involving both prayer and trust can an individual truly let go and surrender. We won't surrender unless we come to know God, and we won't know God if we don't pray. Without this, we'll always be holding back something because we won't trust God enough yet to let it go. Letting go involves letting go spiritually and emotionally of every*thing* else *and* every*one* else in which a person has trusted but which did not bring the person peace. Letting go and surrender do not mean abandonment of people or our responsibilities in life. However, our life or responsibilities could change over time as a result of letting go. Surrender includes giving up trying to find peace or security through anything or anyone other than God. We let go of unhealthy dependency on others. We let go (spiritually or emotionally) of certain things, money, lovers, or whatever else has not brought us the fulfillment we want or desire. The problem is they failed. They failed to bring us the measure of fulfillment, security, and peace our souls were seeking. That's because the peace is God's to give. Out of respect for free will, God waits for a person to trust and surrender before peace comes to the person fully and thereby creates serenity. Similarly, St. Augustine said, "Our hearts were made for God alone, and they will not rest until they rest in God." I'm also reminded of the excellent prayer which came from Alcoholics Anonymous: "God grant me the serenity to accept the things I cannot change, the courage to change the things I can, and the wisdom to know the difference."

To the extent that our ways and lives have not been in keeping with God's ways and love, we've not yet surrendered. It can take a good while. I know I'm not done yet. But at least I've learned the theory. The key with surrender is not trying but *trusting* and giving our lives completely over to the care of God. We trust God based on his Word that he will take good care of us. We can build trust from passages in the Bible such as this: "Which one of you would hand his son a stone when he asks for a loaf of bread, or a snake when he asks for a fish? If you then, who are wicked, know how to give good gifts to your children, how much more will your heavenly Father give good gifts to those who ask him."[167]

Forgiveness

From the very first week of the apparitions, Mary called everyone to "be reconciled" (June 26, 1981). [168] She asked this for the sake of peace, knowing well the tension in relationships all over the world. She wants us to be reconciled with God and with one another. Fighting, conflicts, anger, resentment, and hostilities are so common that unforgiveness is probably the most common stumbling block to one's inner healing and peace. How should we address this? In some cases, we may choose to renew direct contact with someone if we have been divided and hostile. In other cases, we simply need to forgive another within ourselves. If a husband and wife have fought, it's essential to make up in order for the marriage to be fruitful and survive. If two close friends had a fight and aren't talking, somebody has to say words to the effect, "I'm sorry" or "Can we make up?" Otherwise, the friendship will be lost and bad feelings left. In other relationships, no contact is necessary or even helpful. The other person may not be willing to communicate. We may just need to forgive them and move on. They don't want to talk, so it's their issue, not ours. We don't have the power to change others—only God does. Pray for them and move ahead with your life. Let's find positive people for our relationships. Turn problem people over to God. Mary accentuates prayer because she knows the human condition. When we try to change people who can only be changed by God, we fail and get disappointed or hurt. With impossible people, our first, best, and last recourse is to pray to God for them and then let go.

It's only with love and forgiveness for all people with whom we're in relationship that peace is possible. We can't really experience peace if we're blocking grace by a wall of resentment. Jesus made this clear in the Sermon on the Mount when teaching his followers these words of the Our Father: "Forgive us our debts, as we forgive our debtors . . . . If you forgive others their transgressions, your heavenly Father will forgive you. But if you do not forgive others, neither will your Father forgive your transgressions." [169]

Since we can't do it by ourselves, we must ask God for the grace to forgive. At the least, we can make a conscious choice to forgive the one(s) who hurt us. We may also need to forgive God if we're angry at God. You may need to express anger toward God first. If we're angry, God knows that and so we should let it out and say what's in our mind and heart. Sometimes, the hardest person to forgive is our self. Forgiveness is a process that can take either a short time or may last a long time. It depends on how much and how deeply we're hurt. For the deepest scars, it will probably take some significant time to forgive especially grievous offenses. Bitterness is a painful alternative and is the end result of longstanding grudges, harbored and unforgiven. It's not worth it. This can even lead to physical illness in many cases. It's much better to choose forgiveness. What happened may indeed be very significant and we may indeed have been very badly mistreated or even abused, but it's not worth the real estate we may be granting to the offender in our souls. Jesus gave the best example of forgiveness while on the cross. From this place of torment, he prays for his persecutors who put him up there: "Father, forgive them; for they do not know what they are doing" (Luke 23:34, New American Standard Bible).

Conclusion

The Virgin Mary wants our happiness. She's not out to place impossible demands on us. She's not communicated this litany of messages for thirty-one years so that we'll become irritated or spiritually overwhelmed. It's quite the opposite. She'd like for us to be happy and at peace. She wants to *unburden* us. She doesn't pretend that this is an easy road that is without some suffering along the way, but her path leads one on the road of a happy destiny. She said, "I want each one of you to be happy here on earth and to be with me in heaven."[170] That's an important quote and an encouraging statement about the Virgin Mary's intentions in speaking to us for this long at Medjugorje.

Final Words

If I may allude back to the earlier part of this chapter, I was referring to the New England Patriots football team; and the same could be said of the Boston Red Sox, Celtics, Bruins, or any other sports team. Of course, we can go to the games if we want. We can watch them on TV. I watch the baseball play-offs and the World Series each fall. I also watch the National Football League (NFL) play-offs and the Super Bowl. I watched all seven games when the Bruins beat the Vancouver Canucks in hockey during the 2011 Stanley Cup finals. But when the games are over, let's not just do more channel clicking. Let's not make our life all about TV, the Internet, sports, iPads, shopping, etc. Otherwise, we're surely setting ourselves up for grief in this life and in the next. I'm reminded of "hockey parents" fighting it out physically with each other in the stands over their children's game on the ice. That's an example of no surrender, not enough letting go, not putting God first in one's life. Why? Because hockey is first. The children's performance in hockey is first. The parents' pride in their children is first or perhaps it's their desire the child receives a scholarship. If those parents persist that way, they will have much unnecessary grief in this life. (And that doesn't mention the grief caused to the children by creating excessive pressure over athletic competition.) There are many more examples of how a person's clinging to the things of this world so much causes trouble and even disaster. *Now* is the time to resolve these issues. By following the Blessed Virgin's guidance (as described in chapter 5), our lives will change for the better and our needs will be met. This is confirmed in the sixth chapter of Matthew's Gospel in these words of Christ: "But seek first the kingdom of God and His righteousness, and all these things shall be given to you besides" (Matthew 6:33).

The hockey parents, along with the rest of us, can really loosen up if we base our lives on that promise of Christ. This requires conversion. Conversion of our soul is worth more than anything this world can offer. It's worth it eternally. Our road to heaven depends first and foremost on faith in God and salvation in the person of Jesus Christ. Our living out this message of his mother, Mary, will help to strengthen that faith and make us a better and happier person.

Though these are the final words of my twelve chapters on Medjugorje, I really do not have the final words or the final chapter to this story. Just like I did not begin Medjugorje, I cannot end it. This is the final chapter of my book, but it is the hand of God that will write the final chapters of the Medjugorje drama. Medjugorje has the fingerprints of God all over it. He's given us the blueprints for peace, with Mary being sent as principal architect. In Mary's designs, she identifies Jesus as the foundation upon which we should base our faith and spiritual life. I'm the author of this one book, and you will find my fingerprints on the keyboards on which I typed the text. God's fingerprints are on the people and hearts he touched. Our Lady's fingerprints are on the countless people she's prayed for, guided, and consoled, raising us up toward happiness and peace.

Mary, Mother of God and Queen of Peace, thank you for such a generous outpouring of love and for your many words of wisdom. Raise our minds and hearts from this valley of tears to a new promised land of heaven's peace, where Jesus is worshiped in spirit and in truth. Lead us through this desert plain, crossing today's Jordan into a new day, a new land, a new way of doing things, a new life, a renewed and reviving church, and "a new heaven and a new earth."

"Then I saw a new heaven and a new earth. The former heaven and the former earth had passed away, and the sea was no more" (Revelation 21:1).[171]

> Dear children! May your life, anew, be a decision for peace. Be joyful carriers of peace and do not forget that you live in a time of grace, in which God gives you great graces through my presence. Do not close yourselves, little children, but make good use of this time and seek the gift of peace and love for your life so that you may become witnesses to others. I bless you with my motherly blessing. Thank you for having responded to my call. (The Virgin Mary's monthly "Message to the World," given through the visionary Marija Pavlović-Lunetti, September 25, 2008). [172]

Appendix 1

Heaven, Hell, and Purgatory

On November 5, 1981, "four of the Medjugorje visionaries (Vicka, Marija, Ivan, and Jakov) were allowed by Our Lady to see something of hell . . . The Mother of God said that her purpose in giving the visionaries a vista of the gehennal world was to impress upon them the dreadful punishment awaiting sinners who willfully reject her Son's redeeming love and leave this world in that state . . . Some two weeks after that initial experience, Vicka and Jakov were given a more extended view of the place and state of eternal reprobation and torment . . . Vicka has painted a fairly detailed picture of the hellscape she witnessed on two occasions. We find it in the excellent interview with Jan Connell."[173] Please note that the questions and answers written below were excerpted from interviews with the Medjugorje visionaries, Jakov Čolo and Vicka Ivanković—Mijatovic, by the author Jan Connell in her book *Queen of the Cosmos*. In regular print are the questions asked by Ms. Connell. The answers of the visionaries are in italics. Jan Connell's book was published in 1990, nine years following the first reports of the visions in Medjugorje.

Before delving into the very grim and frightening reality of hell, which Jakov and Vicka, especially, illustrate, it is important to point out that according to the Medjugorje revelations, the ones who go to hell are the ones who choose hell as their destination. This point is made very clear in Vicka's explanations. Also, "Marija testifies in similar vein: '*Anyone who goes to hell*,' she quotes the Mother of God as saying, '*does so because they choose it. God does not condemn anyone. They condemn themselves.*'" [174]

From interview with Vicka

What about Hell—is it a place, too?
Yes.

Do many people go there today?
Yes. We saw many people in Hell. Many are there already, and many more will go there when they die.

Why so many?
The Blessed Mother said that those people who are in Hell are there because they chose to go there. They wanted to go to Hell.

Vicka, why would anyone want to go there?
We all know that there are persons on this earth who simply don't admit that God exists, even though He helps them, gives them life and sun and rain and food. He always tries to nudge them onto the path of holiness. They just say they don't believe and they deny Him. They deny Him, even when it is time to die. And they continue to deny Him, even after they are dead. It is their choice. It is their will that they go to Hell. They choose Hell.

Describe Hell as you remember it.
In the center of this place is a great fire, like an ocean of raging flames. We could see people before they went into the fire, and then we could see them coming out of the fire. Before they go into the fire, they look like normal people. The more they are against God's will, the deeper they enter into the fire, and the deeper they go, the more they rage against Him. When they come out of the fire, they don't have human shape anymore; they are more like grotesque animals, but unlike anything on earth. It's as if they were never human beings before.

Can you describe them?
They were horrible. Ugly. Angry. And each was different. No two looked alike.

After they came out of the ocean of fire, what did they do?
When they came out, they were raging and smashing everything around and hissing and gnashing and screeching.

Were you afraid?
I am never afraid when I am with the Blessed Mother. But I didn't like seeing this . . .

When you were there, could you feel the fire's heat?
No, we were in a special grace with the Blessed Mother, so we felt nothing.

Vicka, you said that God condemns no one, that people choose Hell for themselves. Would it be fair to say, then, that if you can choose Hell, you can also choose Heaven?
There are two differences. The people on earth who choose Hell know that they will go there. But no one is sure on the earth if they are going to Heaven or Purgatory. Not one of us is sure.

Can you be sure that you are not going to Hell?
Yes, follow God's will. The most important thing is to know that God loves us.

How does this knowledge help us to go to Heaven?
When we know for sure that God loves us, we try to love Him in return—to respond to God's love for us by being faithful in good times and bad.

Has seeing Hell changed how you pray?
Oh, yes! Now I pray for the conversion of sinners. I know what awaits them if they refuse to convert.

What about Purgatory? Is it near Hell?
First is Heaven, then Purgatory, then Hell. It, too, is a very big space. We couldn't see people in Purgatory—just a misty, gray fog. It looked like ashes. We could sense persons weeping, moaning . . . The Blessed Mother said, "These

people need your prayers, especially the ones that have no one to pray for them."
*And that is why we have prayed so much for these poor souls; they desperately
need our prayers, to go from Purgatory to Heaven!*

Ivan has told pilgrims that the Blessed Mother said souls in
Purgatory . . . can see us on earth . . . during those moments we
pray for them—is that true?
*Yes, they can see us on earth when we pray for them, by name. Please tell people
to pray for their own family members who are dead. Please tell people to pray
and forgive each other, the living and the dead.*

Why is forgiveness so important, Vicka?
Because not to forgive someone hurts us more than the person we won't forgive.

How does this relate to Purgatory?
I am not sure.

What must we do on earth so we don't go to Purgatory when we die?
*I am not sure . . . The Blessed Mother calls us to a holy life. The Bible shows
us how.*[175]

Interview with Jakov

Do you know whether you will go to Heaven when you die?
I have been in Heaven already.

Will you tell us about Heaven?
When you get there, then you will see how it is.

You have said that the reason that the Blessed Mother took you
there was to show you what it would be like for those who remain
faithful to God—would you tell us any more?
If I thought about it too much, I would die of loneliness.

Jakov, have you been in Purgatory?
The Blessed Mother showed Vicka and me Purgatory, but I have not been in it.

You have said that Purgatory is a place where souls are purified. Do you pray for them?
Yes.

Do you suggest that others pray for them?
Yes, as an act of love.

Jakov, did you see Hell?
Yes.

Can you tell us about it?
Very seldom do I talk about Hell.

Why?
I choose not to think about Hell. The self-chosen suffering there is beyond your ability to comprehend.

Does it cause you pain?
More than you can understand.

Why?
Because no one needs to go to Hell. It is the ultimate waste.

What can people do to keep from going to Hell?
Believe in God, no matter what happens in a lifetime. [176]

Appendix 2

Scientific, Psychological, and Theological Studies on the Six Visionaries and the Medjugorje Phenomenon

RESEARCH ON THE VISIONARIES

French-Italian scientific theological commission "on the extraordinary events that are taking place in Medjugorje"

The international French-Italian scientific theological commission "on the extraordinary events that are taking place in Medjugorje" examined the apparitions of Medjugorje the most competently and the most expertly. The assembly of seventeen renowned natural scientists, doctors, psychiatrists and theologians in their research came to a twelve-point conclusion on January 14, 1986, in Paina, near Milan.

1. On the basis of the psychological tests, for all and each of the visionaries it is possible with certainty to exclude fraud and deception.

2. On the basis of the medical examinations, tests and clinical observations etc., for all and each of the visionaries it is possible to exclude pathological hallucinations.

3. On the basis of the results of previous researches for all and each of the visionaries it is possible to exclude a purely natural interpretation of these manifestations.

4. On the basis of information and observations that can be documented, for all and each of the visionaries it is possible to exclude that these manifestations are of the preternatural order i.e. under demonic influence.

5. On the basis of information and observations that can be documented, there is a correspondence between these manifestations and those that are usually described in mystical theology.

6. On the basis of information and observations that can be documented, it is possible to speak of spiritual advances and advances in the theological and moral virtues of the visionaries, from the beginning of these manifestations until today.

7. On the basis of information and observations that can be documented, it is possible to exclude teaching or behavior of the visionaries that would be in clear contradiction to Christian faith and morals.

8. On the basis of information or observations that can be documented, it is possible to speak of good spiritual fruits in people drawn into the supernatural activity of these manifestations and in people favorable to them.

9. After more than four years, the tendencies and different movements that have been generated through Medjugorje,

in consequence of these manifestations, influence the people of God in the Church in complete harmony with Christian doctrine and morals.

10. After more than four years, it is possible to speak of permanent and objective spiritual fruits of movements generated through Medjugorje.

11. It is possible to affirm that all good and spiritual undertakings of the Church, which are in complete harmony with the authentic magisterium of the Church, find support in the events in Medjugorje.

12. Accordingly, one can conclude that after a deeper examination of the protagonists, facts, and their effects, not only in the local framework, but also in regard to the responsive chords of the Church in general, it is well for the Church to recognize the supernatural origin and, thereby, the purpose of the events in Medjugorje.

So far it is the most conscientious and the most complete research of the Medjugorje phenomena, and for that very reason, it is the most positive that has yet been said about it on a scientific-theological level.

French team of experts headed by Mr. Henri Joyeux

A French team of experts headed by Mr. Henri Joyeux also undertook a very serious work of examination of the visionaries. Employing the most modern equipment and expertise, it examined the internal reactions of the visionaries before, during, and after the apparitions. Likewise, the synchronization of their ocular, auditory, cardiac, and cerebral reactions. The results of that commission were very significant. They showed that the object of observation is external to the visionaries and that any external manipulation or mutual agreement between the visionaries is excluded. The results with individual electro-encephalograms and other reactions are collected and elaborated in a special book (H. Joyeux, R. Laurentin, *Etudes medicales et scientifique sur les Apparitions de Medjugorje*, Paris 1986).

The results of the last mentioned commission confirmed the conclusions of the international commission, and for their part, they proved that the apparitions, to which the visionaries testify, are a phenomenon that surpasses modern science and that all points toward some other level of happening.

INSTITUTE FOR THE FIELD LIMITS OF SCIENCE (IGW)—INNSBRUCK

CENTRE FOR STUDY AND RESEARCH ON PSYCHOPHYSIOLOGY OF STATES OF CONSCIOUSNESS—MILANO

EUROPEAN SCHOOL OF HYPNOTIC PSYCHOTHERAPY AMISI OF MILAN

PARAPSYCHOLOGY CENTER OF BOLOGNA.

At the request of the Parish Office of Medugorje, psycho-physiological and psycho-diagnostic research was carried out on the subjects who since 1981 are known as the visionaries' group of Medugorje.

The research was carried out in four sessions:

- The first research was carried out on April 22-23, 1998, at the Casa Incontri Cristiani (House of Christian Encounters) in Capiago Intimiano (Como), which is operated by the Dehonian Fathers. On this occasion the examined were: Ivan Dragićević, Marija Pavlović-Lunetti, and Vicka Ivanković.

- The second research was carried out from on July 23-24, 1998, in Međugorje. Examined were Mirjana Soldo-Dragićević, Vicka Ivanković and Ivanka Elez-Ivanković.

- The third research, only psycho-diagnostic, was conducted by psychologist Lori Bradvica on Jakov Čolo with the collaboration of Fr. Ivan Landeka.

- The fourth psycho-physiological registration was conducted December 11, 1998, in the same House of Christian Encounters in Capiago Intimiano (Como) with Marija Pavlović.

The incompleteness of the psycho-physiological investigation was caused by the partial cooperation of some subjects who did not undergo what the working group had expected, due either to their family or social obligations or to their personal reluctance, even though Fr. Slavko Barbarić and Fr. Ivan Landeka encouraged them to do it, without any influences on the programs of the working group called "Međugorje 3," because, apart from individual medical or psychological investigation, prior to this research two groups had operated: the first a group of French doctors in 1984, and the second a group of Italian doctors in 1985. In addition three European psychiatrists in 1986 carried out only psychiatric-diagnostic investigations.

The following collaborated in the "Međugorje 3" work group:

- Fr. Andreas Resch, theologian and psychologist from Institute for the Field Limits of Science (IGW)—Innsbruck; General coordinator.

- Dr. Giorgio Gagliardi, medical psycho-physiologist from the Centre for Study and Research on Psychophysiology of States of Consciousness—Milano; member of board

179

of European School of Hypnotic Psychotherapy AMISI, Milan and of the Parapsychology Centre of Bologna.

- Dr. Marco Margnelli, medical psycho-physiologist and neuro-physiologist from the Centre for Study and Research on States of Consciousness—Milano, member of the professors' board of the European School AMISI, Milan;

- Dr. Mario Cigada, psychotherapist and oculist, Milano, member of the professorial board of the European School AMISI, Milano;

- Dr. Luigi Ravagnati, neurologist; assistant for neuro-surgery at the University of Milan, member of the professors' board of the European School of Hypnotic Psychotherapy AMISI, Milan

- Dr. Marianna Bolko, psychiatrist and psychoanalyst, instructor for specialization in psychotherapy at the University of Bologna.

- Dr. Virginio Nava, psychiatrist; head doctor at Como Psychiatric Hospital.

- Dr. Rosanna Constantini, psychologist, instructor at Auxilium University, Rome.

- Dr. Fabio Alberghina, medical internist.

- Dr. Giovanni Li Rosi, gynecologist at Varese Hospital and specialist for hypnotic psychotherapy, AMISI, Milan.

- Dr. Gaetano Perriconi, internist at FBF Hospital in Erbi/ Como.

- Prof. Massimo Pagani, medical internist, professor of internal medicine at the University of Milan.

- Dr. Gabriella Raffaelli, scientific secretary;

- Fiorella Gagliardi, secretary, community assistant.

The following tests were used on the subjects to investigate their actual psychophysical and psychological situation:

- Complete case history,

- Medical case history,

- MMPI, EPI, MHQ; Tree test, Person test, Raven Matrixes, Rorschach Test, Hand test, Valsecchi truth and lie detection test;

- Neurological visit,

- Computerized polygraph (skin electrical activity; peripheral cardiac capillary and heartbeat activities; skeletal and diaphragmatic pneumography) during the apparitional experience, during mediated hypnotic recall of the same apparitional experience.

- Holter's arterial pressure dynamic registration.

- Holter's electro-cardiographic /respiratory dynamic registration.

- Pupillary reflexes (photomotor) and winking reflex

- Video tapes

- Photographs.

For all the tests performed the visionaries made their decision with full freedom, readiness, and collaboration.

The results from these psychological-diagnostic investigations show that:

During the period since age 17, from the beginning of their apparitional experiences, the subjects do not exhibit any kind of pathological symptoms like trance interference, disassociate interference and loss of reality interference.

All subjects investigated, however, exhibited symptoms that are related to justified stress that occurs through very high levels of exogenous and endogenous stimulation as a consequence of everyday life.

From their personal testimonies it follows that the initial and subsequent altered state of consciousness occurs due to their unusual experiences that they themselves recognize and define and still continuously recognize as a vision/apparition of Our Lady.

The psychophysical investigation was carried out on four states of consciousness:

- Waking state;

- Altered state of consciousness (hypnosis with investigation of the state of ecstasy);

- State of visualization of mental images;

- Altered state of consciousness (defined as the ecstasy of apparition).

The aim was to investigate whether the ecstatic state of apparition, already registered in 1985 by the Italian doctors working group, still continues to be present or has undergone changes. In addition it was desired to investigate potential coincidence/divergence with other states off consciousness such as guided visualization or hypnosis.

Results of the investigation carried out demonstrate that the ecstatic phenomenology can be compared to the one from 1985 with somewhat less intensity.

The hypnotically induced state of ecstasy did not cause the phenomenology of spontaneous experiences and therefore it can be deduced that the ecstatic states of spontaneous apparitions were not states of hypnotic trance.

Capiago Intimiano, December 12, 1998
                    Undersigned:
                    Fr. Andreas Resch, Dr. Giorgio Gagliardi, Dr. Marco Margnelli, Dr. Marianna Bolko, Dr. Gabriella Raffaelli.

All information for this appendix taken from www.medjugorje.hr, Information Centre "MIR" Medjugorje.[177]

Appendix 3

Additional Statements of the Church on Matters Concerning Medjugorje

All information and statements presented in this appendix come from the Information Center and official website for: **Medjugorje: Place of Peace and Reconciliation.** The website is managed on location in Medjugorje and is monitored by the Franciscan priests who run the local parish, Saint James Church. It is www. medjugorje.hr

Before reading the statements in this appendix, a short introduction would be beneficial. Below you will find a series of written statements made first by bishops within the former Yugoslavia, followed by statements made by the Vatican Congregation for the Doctrine of the Faith (CDF) and also statements from a Vatican spokesperson acting in an official capacity for the church's Holy See. These statements address a number of different questions regarding the Medjugorje event, including the question of whether the church views the visions as authentic and supernatural, the status of the investigations, the issue of making pilgrimage there, and some other important matters, such as the position of the current bishop of the diocese of Mostar, Ratko Perić. Regarding the issue of pilgrimage, Dr. Navarro-Valls's 1996 communications, representing the Holy See, clarified that the faithful may go to Medjugorje on pilgrimage, and they may be accompanied by a priest, if they wish one to be present.

It is my understanding, based on the last letter in this section (from the Congregation for the Doctrine of the Faith) that the Vatican still upholds the *Declaration at Zadar* as the church's most official position until and unless things change or develop further. The same 1998 letter, as explained by Archbishop Bertone, confirms and clarifies that Rome gave authority to the wider body of local bishops in the country of Bosnia and Herzegovina to address the Medjugorje question. Ordinarily, Rome gives solely to the local bishop of a diocese the authority to make conclusions on matters pertaining to private revelations. In this exceptional situation, however, the opinions of the local bishop (of Mostar) are identified by Archbishop Bertone as just that, his opinions. It is clear that Rome wanted all of the bishops of that country to weigh in on the final conclusions and determinations made about Medjugorje and renew the process of the investigations as they saw fit. This shift began in 1987 when (then) Cardinal Ratzinger rejected a negative 1986 report on Medjugorje issued by the former bishop of Mostar (Msgr. Pavao Žanić). Accordingly, it was originally then that Rome removed the Medjugorje dossier from the exclusive domain of the Mostar bishop and gave it to all of his contemporary bishops of the country, first being throughout Yugoslavia but then throughout Bosnia-Herzegovina following the civil war. It appears that these bishops will not be the ones who issue further official declarations about Medjugorje. As explained in chapter 11, the Vatican took over the work of investigation on this matter in March 2010. An International Commission has been formed which is responsible for making a report to the Vatican. Cardinal Camilio Ruini was appointed by the Holy See to head this commission. Their work is ongoing and they have interviewed each of the visionaries in Rome as part of their work. They're expected to issue a report by the end of 2012.

With that as an introduction, the first statement is printed below. The Declaration at Zadar, made in 1991, remains the official position of the Catholic Church until a more definitive position and declaration is made. The Declaration at Zadar is an official but not a final determination, as the wording leaves open the possibility to review and reevaluate matters as things progress. Immediately below the declaration is a commentary by the Catholic-Croatian newspaper *Glas Koncila.* Following *Glas Konica's* commentary, all the remaining statements are from the Vatican (e.g., representing the Holy See).

DECLARATION OF THE EX-YUGOSLAVIA BISHOPS' CONFERENCE ON MEDJUGORJE

At the ordinary session of the Bishops' Conference of Yugoslavia in Zadar from April 9-11, 1991, the following was adopted:

DECLARATION

The bishops, from the very beginning, have been following the events of Medjugorje through the Bishop of the diocese (Mostar), the Bishop's Commission and the Commission of the Bishops Conference of Yugoslavia on Medjugorje.

On the basis of the investigations, so far it cannot be affirmed that one is dealing with supernatural apparitions and revelations.

However, the numerous gatherings of the faithful from different parts of the world, who come to Medjugorje, prompted both by motives of belief and various other motives, require the attention and pastoral care in the first place of the diocesan bishop and with him of the other bishops also, so that in Medjugorje and in everything connected with it a healthy devotion to the Blessed Virgin Mary may be promoted in accordance with the teaching of the Church.

For this purpose, the bishops will issue especially suitable liturgical-pastoral directives. Likewise, through their Commission they will continue to keep up with and investigate the entire event in Medjugorje.

In Zadar April 10, 1991
The Bishops of Yugoslavia

ON MEDJUGORJE—SOMETHING MORE DEFINITE

Editorial Commentary in Glas Koncila, *official national Croatian Catholic newspaper, Zagreb, May 5, 1991, p. 2*

The latest declaration on Medjugorje from the Catholic Bishops of the Socialist Federal Republic of Yugoslavia is a classic example of the centuries old practice of authentic ecclesiastical prudence. It demonstrates that the Church respects facts above all, that it carefully measures its competence and that in all matters it is mostly concerned for the spiritual welfare of the faithful.

It is a fact known to the whole world that, because of news about Our Lady's apparitions already for a full ten years, both believing and inquisitive people have been gathering in Medjugorje. Is it a fact that the Mother of God is really appearing there and giving messages? The Bishops, carefully holding to their competency, declare, "On the basis of investigations so far it cannot be affirmed."

The content and the sense of that declaration have to be considered on two levels. In this case, the first and the essential level is that the contents of such possible so-called private revelations cannot be added to the revealed and obligatory contents of the faith.

Therefore, neither the Bishops nor the Pope himself have the authority either to conclude infallibly that Our Lady has really appeared somewhere or the authority to impose on the faithful to believe that she has appeared. The Magisterium of the Church is infallible under well-known conditions only when it affirms that something is contained or not contained in that Revelation which the Church received up to the end of the apostolic age and which is preserved in Scripture and Tradition. Whatever is not included, neither in Scripture nor in Tradition the Magisterium cannot proclaim as a doctrine of the faith nor as content to be believed under obligation. Accordingly, only the uninstructed could expect the Bishops to resolve the question of the Medjugorje apparitions for us so as then to know exactly what we are allowed or not allowed to believe about them.

But on the other hand then why are they so carefully investigating that report? Because they do have the obligation to establish whether that which is taking place there and is being proclaimed from there is in accordance with the entirety of the revealed truth of the faith and of moral doctrine. If it is established that there is nothing contrary, that the revelations and messages are in accordance with Catholic faith and morals, they, as the most responsible in the Church, could proclaim that there is neither any objection to gatherings of the faithful in that place nor to the development of the spiritual life according to the sense of those messages. On the contrary, it would be their obligation to expose errors and prevent abuses. The pertinent expressions in the new Declaration show that the investigations are also continuing in that sense.

But the main force of the Declaration shows that our bishops are above all taking notice of the factual gathering of a large number of the faithful and of the inquisitive in Medjugorje and they consider it their duty to insure that such a large number of gatherings there receive a correct proclamation of the faith, an orthodox and up-to-date catechesis, so that the holy sacraments are correctly and worthily administered there and especially that the Medjugorje

Marian devotion develops in accord with Christian orthodoxy. That position is the real news of this document.

Surely, as the document itself states, one should expect suitable liturgical-pastoral directives for the solemn celebrations in Medjugorje. A proposal made long ago, which was also emphasized in *Glas Koncila*, would also thereby be realized, namely, that the bishops' care for Medjugorje be divided between two commissions, One would continue investigating whether there are or are not supernatural apparitions or revelations, and the other would take care of the proper and healthy ecclesiastical conduct of the Medjugorje gatherings. This is because it is really possible that the first of these commissions would still be investigating for a long time and maybe even decide not to publish its final opinion, whereas care for the gatherings cannot be postponed because they are continuously taking place.

For many devout people around the whole world this Declaration will serve as a valuable relief in the area of conscience. Those, namely, who come to Medjugorje motivated by belief, will from now on know that those gatherings are covered by the ordinary and responsible care of the successors of the apostles.

A FRENCH BISHOP AND VATICAN CONGREGATION ON MEDJUGORJE

The bishop of Langres in France, Msgr. Leon Taverdet, took recourse to the Apostolic See February 14, 1996, to ask what the position of the church is regarding the apparitions in Medjugorje and whether it is permitted to go there for pilgrimage. The Holy See's Sacred Congregation for the Doctrine of the Faith answered March 23, 1996, through its secretary archbishop, Tarcisio Bertone. We present his response in its entirety.

SACRED CONGREGATION FOR THE DOCTRINE OF THE FAITH

Vatican City, March 23, 1996
Prot. No. 154/81-01985

Your Excellency,

In your letter of February 14, 1996, you inquired what is the present position of the Church regarding the alleged "apparitions in Medjugorje" and whether it is permitted to the Catholic faith to go there for pilgrimage.

In reference to that, it is my honour to make known to you that, regarding the authenticity of the apparitions in question, the Bishops of the former Yugoslavia confirmed in their Declaration of April 10, 1991 published in Zadar:

"On the basis of investigation up till now it cannot be established that one is dealing with supernatural apparitions and revelations.

However, the numerous gatherings of the faithful from different parts of the world, who are coming to Medjugorje prompted both by motives of belief and certain other motives, require the attention and pastoral care in the first place of the bishop of the diocese and of the other bishops with him so that in Medjugorje and everything related to it a healthy devotion toward the Blessed Virgin Mary would be promoted in conformity with the teaching of the Church.

For that purpose, the bishops shall issue separate appropriate liturgical-pastoral directives. Likewise by means of their Commission they shall further follow and investigate the total event in Medjugorje."

The result from this in what is precisely said is that official pilgrimages to Medjugorje, understood as a place of authentic Marian apparitions, are not permitted to be organized either on the parish or on the diocesan level, because that would be in contradiction to what the Bishops of former Yugoslavia affirmed in their fore mentioned Declaration.

Kindly accept, your Excellency, an expression of my profoundly devoted affection!

+ Tarcisio Bertone

THE LATEST VATICAN STATEMENT ABOUT MEDJUGORJE

From the beginning of June 1996, many of the public means of communication reported that the Vatican had prohibited pilgrimages to Medjugorje. Spokesman for the Holy See, Joaquin Navarro-Valls, immediately refuted this. However, in case there would remain any doubt regarding the stance of the Vatican toward Medjugorje, the spokesman for the Holy See clarified their position once again. Here we treat of the subject in full:

INDIVIDUALS PERMITTED TO VISIT MEDJUGORJE

By Catholic News Service

While the Vatican has never said that Catholics may not go to Medjugorje, it has told bishops that their parishes and dioceses may not organise official pilgrimages to the site of the alleged Marian apparitions, the Vatican spokesman said.

"You cannot say people cannot go there until it has been proven false. This has not been said, so anyone can go if they want," the spokesman, Joaquin Navarro-Valls, told Catholic News Service Aug. 21.

In addition, he said, when Catholic faithful go anywhere, they are entitled to spiritual care, so the church does not forbid priests to accompany lay-organized trips to Medjugorje in Bosnia-Herzegovina, just as it would not forbid them accompanying a group of Catholics visiting South Africa.

Navarro-Valls insisted, "nothing has changed" regarding the Vatican's position on Medjugorje.

In early June, a French newspaper published excerpts from a letter about Medjugorje pilgrimages written by the secretary of the Vatican Congregation for the Doctrine of the Faith in response to a question from a French bishop.

The letter from Archbishop Tarcisio Bertone of the doctrinal congregation quoted from a 1991 statement by the bishops of former Yugoslavia, which said that after much study, "it cannot be confirmed that supernatural apparitions or revelations are occurring here."

"However," the bishops said—and Archbishop Bertone repeated—"the number of the faithful travelling to Medjugorje requires for the church to arrange for their pastoral care."

After quoting the 1991 statement, Archbishop Bertone wrote, "From what was said, it follows that official pilgrimages to Medjugorje, understood as a place of authentic Marian apparitions, should not be organised either on a parish or diocesan level because it would be in contradiction with what the bishops of ex-Yugoslavia said in their declaration cited above."

Navarro-Valls said, "When one reads what Archbishop Bertone wrote, one could get the impression that from now on everything is prohibited, no possibility" for Catholics to travel to Medjugorje.

But, in fact, "nothing has changed, nothing new has been said," the spokesman told CNS.

"The problem is if you systematically organize pilgrimages, organize them with the bishop and the church, you are giving a canonical sanction to the facts of Medjugorje," which the church is still in the process of studying.

"This is different from people going in a group who bring a priest with them in order to go to confession," the spokesman said.

Navarro-Valls said he commented because "I was worried that what Archbishop Bertone said could be interpreted in too restricted a way. Has the church or the Vatican said no to Medjugorje? No."

STATEMENT OF THE DIRECTOR OF THE PRESS OFFICE OF THE HOLY SEE, DR. JOAQUIN NAVARRO-VALLS, ON PILGRIMAGE TO MEDJUGORJE

No new fact has been undertaken regarding this.

As has been already stated on previous occasions, in these cases respect of the immediate competence of the local episcopate is required.

In regard to that, on April 10, 1991 the Bishops of ex-Yugoslavia declared: "On the basis of the investigations, so far it cannot be affirmed that one is dealing with supernatural apparitions and revelations. However, the numerous gatherings of the faithful from different parts of the world, who come to Medjugorje prompted both by motives of belief and various other motives, require attention and pastoral care in the first place of the bishop of the diocese and with him of the other bishops also, so that in Medjugorje and in everything connected with it a healthy devotion to the Blessed Virgin Mary may be promoted in accordance with the teaching of the Church."

One must still repeatedly emphasize the indispensable necessity of continuing the search and the reflection, besides the prayer, in the face of any presumed supernatural phenomenon, as long as there be no definitive pronouncement.

Bolletino No. 233—June 19, 1996

CONGREGATIO PRO DOCTRINA FIDEI ON MEDJUGORJE

CONGREGATIO PRO DOCTRINA FIDEI

CITTA DEL VATICANO, PALAZZO DEL S. UFFIZIO
Pr. No 154/81-06419
May 26, 1998
To His Excellency Mons. Gilbert Aubry,
Bishop of Saint-Denis de la Reunion

Excellency,

In your letter of January 1, 1998, you submitted to this Dicastery several questions about the position of the Holy See and of the Bishop of Mostar in regard to the so-called apparitions of Medjugorje, private pilgrimages and the pastoral care of the faithful who go there.

In regard to this matter, I think it is impossible to reply to each of the questions posed by Your Excellency. The main thing I would like to point out is that the Holy See does not ordinarily take a position of its own regarding supposed supernatural phenomena as a court of first instance. As for the credibility of the "apparitions" in question, this Dicastery respects what was decided by the bishops of the former Yugoslavia in the Declaration of Zadar, April 10, 1991: *"On the basis of the investigations so far, it cannot be affirmed that one is dealing with supernatural apparitions and revelations."* Since the division of Yugoslavia into different independent nations, it would now pertain to the members of the Episcopal Conference of Bosnia-Herzegovina to eventually reopen the examination of this case, and to make any new pronouncements that might be called for.

What Bishop Perić said in his letter to the Secretary General of "Famille Chretienne," declaring: *"My conviction and my position is not only 'non constat de supernaturalitate,' but likewise, 'constat de non supernaturalitate' of the apparitions or revelations in Medjugorje,"* should be considered the expression of the personal conviction of the Bishop of Mostar which he has the right to express as Ordinary of the place, but which is and remains his personal opinion.

Finally, as regards pilgrimages to Medjugorje, which are conducted privately, this Congregation points out that they are permitted on condition that they are not regarded as an authentication of events still taking place and which still call for an examination by the Church.

I hope that I have replied satisfactorily at least to the principal questions that you have presented to this Dicastery and I beg Your Excellency to accept the expression of my devoted sentiments.

Archbishop Tarcisio Bertone

(Secretary to the "Congregation for the Doctrine," presided over by Cardinal Ratzinger)

This is the summary of the letter:

1. *The declarations of the Bishop of Mostar only reflect his personal opinion. Consequently, they are not an official and definitive judgment from the Church.*

2. *One is directed to the Declaration of Zadar, which leaves the door open to future investigations. In the meanwhile, private pilgrimages with pastoral accompaniment for the faithful are permitted.*

3. *A new commission could eventually be named.*

4. *In the meanwhile, all Catholics may go as pilgrims to Medjugorje. We can't but be thankful for this long awaited explanation.*

p. Daniel-Ange

Reference for all statements printed in appendix 3: [178]

Appendix 4

How to Pray the Rosary

The rosary has been hailed by sinners and saints alike as a powerful prayer to God. It is a most effective means for repelling the attacks of the devil and his agents. Beautiful in its simplicity and its biblical mysteries, the rosary can take its reciter to a high spiritual plain. It can immediately bring one into contact with the Virgin Mary, who, in turn, brings the Holy Spirit into our midst and soul. The Holy Spirit comes to the person who begins to pray the Hail Mary with devotion, as the Spirit finds the sound of this repeated prayer most pleasing. Not long after reciting the decades, a person can easily pass from anxious concern or distress to a place of relaxed meditation. Some patience and level of commitment is essential to get started. One should not get discouraged merely due to the inability to complete the fifty-three Hail Marys on the beads. The grace is God's to give, which we either have or do not have. If you cannot do the five decades, complete three. If you cannot complete three, complete two. Keep coming back to it each day and trying until you can pray a whole rosary. You have an excellent Christian advantage in the struggles of life if you can pray the rosary (five decades) at least one time each day. With more grace, you could try ten or fifteen decades. Actually, at Medjugorje, the Blessed Virgin has asked that we try to do fifteen decades a day. I now proceed with the specific instructions.

The Holy Rosary: Step-by-Step Instructions for Praying the Rosary

(Just beneath the instructions are all the words to each of the prayers. Next, you will see a diagram of a typical rosary.)

I.   Beginning with the rosary's cross, begin by saying, "In the name of the Father and of the Son and of the Holy Spirit" (making the sign of the cross while doing that). Then pray the Apostles' Creed. This and all prayers of the rosary are meditative prayers.

II. On the single bead just above the cross, pray the Our Father.

III. The next cluster of beads comprises three beads. The Hail Mary prayer is said on these three beads. You pray the three Hail Marys while meditating on three divine virtues of faith, hope, and love/charity.

IV. On the next bead, which is a single bead, you pray the Glory Be.

V.   Then announce the first divine mystery of contemplation. For example, if it was a Monday, you would say the first Joyful Mystery is the Annunciation. Then while beginning to contemplate the mystery, you pray the Our Father prayer.

VI. Now this will bring you to the first decade or set of ten beads of the rosary. You will then pray ten Hail Marys while continuing to contemplate the first mystery (e.g., of The Annunciation).

VII. After the tenth Hail Mary you will have completed the first of five decades that make up a chaplet of the rosary.

You now come to another single bead. At this point, you pray the Glory Be and then (on the same bead) pray the O My Jesus and then (on the same bead) announce the next or second mystery. For example, if it's Monday and you're praying the Joyful Mysteries, you say, "The second Joyful Mystery is the Visitation." At this point you pray the Our Father.

VIII. You will now come to the second decade or group of ten beads; you will now pray ten Hail Marys again while contemplating the appropriate mystery.

IX. You continue to pray the rosary the same way throughout. If your intention is to pray a chaplet (a single set of five mysteries) at the end of the fifth mystery you will come back to the joiner. This is where the decades all join with the lower part of the rosary, which contains the cross. When you come to the joiner, you decide whether or not you wish to say another chaplet or end. If you decide to say another chaplet you simply announce the next mystery and continue. If you wish to end, you simply say the Glory Be to the Father and the O My Jesus and end the rosary with the Hail Holy Queen and then, again, the sign of the cross.

Various prayers in approximate order as prayed in the rosary

THE APOSTLE'S CREED: I believe in God, the Father Almighty, Creator of heaven and earth and in Jesus Christ, his only Son, our Lord, who was conceived by the Holy Spirit, born of the Virgin Mary, suffered under Pontius Pilate, was crucified, died, and was buried. He descended into hell; the third day he arose again from the dead. He ascended into heaven, sitteth at the right hand of God, the Father Almighty, from thence he shall come to judge the living and the dead. I believe in the Holy Spirit, the Holy Catholic Church, the Communion of saints, the forgiveness of sins, the resurrection of the body, and life everlasting. Amen.

THE OUR FATHER: Our Father, who art in heaven, hallowed be thy name; thy kingdom come, thy will be done on earth as it is in heaven. Give us this day our daily bread and forgive us our trespasses as we forgive those who trespass against us and lead us not into temptation but deliver us from evil. Amen.

THE DOXOLOGY (or GLORY BE): Glory be to the Father, the Son, and the Holy Spirit. As it was in the beginning is now and ever shall be, world without end. Amen. (This prayer is optional and may be said after all Glory Be to the Fathers.)

O MY JESUS: Oh my Jesus, forgive us our sins. Save us from the fires of hell. Lead all souls to heaven, especially those most in need of thy mercy. Amen.

THE HAIL MARY: Hail Mary, full of grace, the Lord is with thee, blessed art thou amongst women and blessed is the fruit of thy womb, Jesus. Holy Mary, Mother of God, pray for us sinners now and at the hour of our death. Amen.

OPTIONAL PRAYER TO BE ADDED AT THE END OF EACH DECADE (prayer for priests): God, our Father, please send us more holy priests, all for the Sacred and Eucharistic heart of Jesus, all for the sorrowful and Immaculate Heart of Mary, in union with Saint Joseph. Amen.

PRAYERS AT THE CONCLUSION OF THE ROSARY CHAPLET:

THE SALVE REGINA (HAIL HOLY QUEEN): Hail Holy Queen, Mother of Mercy, our life our sweetness and our hope. To thee do we cry, poor banished children of Eve; to thee do we send up our sighs, mourning, and weeping in this valley of tears. Turn then, most gracious advocate, thine eyes of mercy toward us and after this our exile show unto us the blessed fruit of thy womb, Jesus. O clement, O loving, O sweet Virgin Mary!

V: Pray for us, O Holy Mother of God

R: That we may be made worthy of the promises of Christ.

LET US PRAY (ADDITIONAL PRAYER AT END OF ROSARY): O God, by the life, death, and resurrection of your only Son, you purchased for us the rewards of eternal life; grant, we beseech you that while meditating on these mysteries of the most holy rosary, we may imitate what they contain and obtain what they promise. Through the same Christ our Lord. Amen.

FATIMA PRAYER (OPTIONAL): Most Holy Trinity—Father, Son, and Holy Spirit—I adore thee profoundly. I offer thee the most precious body, blood, soul, and divinity of Jesus Christ, present in all the tabernacles of the world, in reparation for the outrages, sacrileges, and indifferences whereby he is offended. And through the infinite merits of his most Sacred Heart and the Immaculate Heart of Mary, I beg of thee the conversion of poor sinners.

"Let this prayer be echoed all over the world."—Mary

FATIMA PRAYER #2 (OPTIONAL): My God, I believe, I adore, I hope, and I love you. I beg pardon of you for those who do not believe, do not adore, do not hope, and do not love you.

Mary, Queen of the Holy Rosary, pray for us. Mary, Queen of Peace, pray for us. Mary, Our Loving Mother, pray for us.

MEMORARE: Remember, O most gracious Virgin Mary that never was it known that anyone who fled to your protection, implored your help, or sought your intercession was left unaided. Inspired with this confidence, we fly to you, O Virgin of virgins, our Mother. To you we come; before you we stand, sinful and sorrowful. O Mother of the Word Incarnate, despise not our petitions but, in your mercy, hear and answer us. Amen.

An image of a typical rosary is just below.

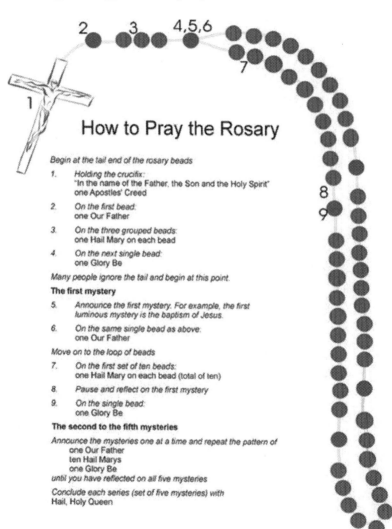

How to Pray the Rosary

Begin at the tail end of the rosary beads

1. Holding the crucifix:
   "In the name of the Father, the Son and the Holy Spirit"
   one Apostles' Creed

2. On the first bead:
   one Our Father

3. On the three grouped beads:
   one Hail Mary on each bead

4. On the next single bead:
   one Glory Be

Many people ignore the tail and begin at this point.

The first mystery

5. Announce the first mystery. For example, the first luminous mystery is the baptism of Jesus.

6. On the same single bead as above:
   one Our Father

Move on to the loop of beads

7. On the first set of ten beads:
   one Hail Mary on each bead (total of ten)

8. Pause and reflect on the first mystery

9. On the single bead:
   one Glory Be

The second to the fifth mysteries

Announce the mysteries one at a time and repeat the pattern of
   one Our Father
   ten Hail Marys
   one Glory Be
until you have reflected on all five mysteries

Conclude each series (set of five mysteries) with
Hail, Holy Queen

The Fifteen Promises of Mary to Christians Who Recite the Rosary

- Whoever shall faithfully serve me by the recitation of the rosary shall receive signal graces.

- I promise my special protection and the greatest graces to all those who shall recite the rosary.

- The rosary shall be a powerful armor against hell; it will destroy vice, decrease sin, and defeat heresies.

- It will cause virtue and good works to flourish; it will obtain for souls the abundant mercy of God; it will withdraw the heart of men from the love of the world and its vanities, and will lift them to the desire of eternal things. Oh, that souls would sanctify themselves by this means.

- The soul that recommends itself to me by the recitation of the rosary shall not perish.

- Whoever shall recite the rosary devoutly, applying himself to the consideration of its sacred mysteries shall never be conquered by misfortune. God will not chastise him in His justice, he shall not die by an unprovided death; if he be just he shall remain in the grace of God, and become worthy of eternal life.

- Whoever shall have a true devotion for the rosary shall not die without the sacraments of the Church.

- Those who are faithful to recite the rosary shall have during their life and at their death the light of God and the plenitude of His graces; at the moment of death they shall participate in the merits of the saints in paradise.

- I shall deliver from purgatory those who have been devoted to the rosary.

- The faithful children of the rosary shall merit a high degree of glory in heaven.

- You shall obtain all you ask of me by the recitation of the rosary.

- All those who propagate the holy rosary shall be aided by me in their necessities.

- I have obtained from my Divine Son that all the advocates of the rosary shall have for intercessors the entire celestial court during their life and at the hour of death.

- All who recite the rosary are my son, and brothers of my only son Jesus Christ.

- Devotion of my rosary is a great sign of predestination.

(Given to St. Dominic and Blessed Alan Imprimatur: Patrick J. Hayes DD, former Archbishop of New York)

WHY THE DAILY ROSARY?

- Our Lady has 117 titles. She selected this title at Fatima: "I am the Lady of the Rosary."

- St. Francis de Sales said the greatest method of praying *is* Pray the Rosary.

- St. Thomas Aquinas preached 40 straight days in Rome Italy on just the Hail Mary.

- St. John Vianney, patron of priests, was seldom seen without a rosary in his hand.

- "The rosary is the scourge of the devil"—Pope Adrian VI

- "The rosary is a treasure of graces"—Pope Paul V

- Saint Padre Pio, the stigmatic priest said, "The Rosary is *the weapon.*"

- Pope Leo XIII wrote 9 encyclicals on the rosary.

- Pope John XXIII spoke 38 times about Our Lady and the Rosary. He prayed 15 decades daily.

- St. Louis Marie Grignion de Montfort wrote, "The rosary is the most powerful weapon to touch the Heart of Jesus, Our Redeemer, who so loves His Mother."

- MARY, QUEEN OF THE HOLY ANGELS, PRAY FOR US!

- "Jesus, Mary, I Love You, Save Souls"

- JMJ = JESUS, MARY, and JOSEPH—the Holy Family . . .

Reference: See note [179]

Appendix 5

Theology of Private Revelations

Author's note: In this analysis, Father Svetozar Kraljevic, OFM, quotes the renowned Jesuit priest and author Karl Rahner (1904-1984) several times on the topic of apparitions and other private revelations, as well as on their meaning and significance in the life of the Church (Father Svetozar's statements are in double quotations ["] while Karl Rahner's are in single quotations [']).

"Theology, because it is in the service of the Church, must recognize God's salvific work in the world which is always the continuation of what began in the Old Testament and was completed for all time in Jesus Christ. 'Therefore the essence of all private revelations after Christ must be such as to fit into this eschatological and salvific reality'" (Karl Rahner, SJ [1958], *Visionen und Prophezeiungen*, p.26).

"The Church is called to put spirits to a test to see if they belong to God (1 John 4:1)—or whether they turn the faithful from worshiping Jesus Christ and, instead, place Mary at the center of devotion, in competition with Christ. This calling, therefore, also pertains to assessing the criteria of visionaries and their purported experiences."

"Theology classifies apparitions in two categories: the mystical and the prophetic. The former is exclusively for the person in question, for his or her growth in the spiritual life. The latter takes the form of a gift (to either an individual or a group) for the public benefit—for the benefit of the whole Church. Mystical apparitions are more intense and lead to a deeper spiritual experience of God, whereas prophetic apparitions do not necessarily have as strong an influence on the person or persons; change is slower in the sense of holiness of life."

"For example, the revelation at Lourdes is authentic and is directed to the whole Church but it is still, theologically considered, a *private* revelation and belief in it is not obligatory for the faithful—as distinguished from the *public* revelation contained in the Bible and the Tradition of the Church which is obligatory."

"Logically, according to Karl Rahner, there is no difference in essence between private and public revelation. In God, there is no *essential* and *less essential revelation*; every word from Him is essential for the salvation of man. 'The act of faith is connatural with the fact that God has spoken publicly through Jesus Christ or privately through the prophet He has chosen'" (Rahner, *Visionen und Prophezeiungen*, p. 24).

"The intent of private revelation is not to teach the faithful different meanings of existing truths; its imperative meaning 'is to help Christianity act in a particular historic situation' (Rahner, *Visionen und Prophezeiungen*, p.27). The *matter* of private revelations is specific and practical advice that God directs to His Church when she finds herself in a situation where all other means are exhausted. Thus, we conclude with Rahner, 'Contrary to the fact that the revelation is ended, the prophetic element in the Church has its significance which cannot be substituted or replaced by the theological theory, human wisdom, and understanding of the Church's teaching authority and mysticism' (Rahner, *Visionen und Prophezeiungen*, p. 30). The Church would ignore this voice to her detriment."

"When this voice is not completely clear, the Church together with Mary asks, 'How can this be?' (Luke 1:34). For Mary, certainty sprang from her candor and her obedience to God. The Church, in these circumstances, can only be open to the incentives of the Holy Spirit, while using all means for the discernment of spirits."

"How does one prove the authenticity of the apparitions? The goal and the duty of investigation are to ascertain if such occurrences are products of the imagination and subjective experiences of the alleged visionaries. It cannot be presumed that visions are objective or 'natural'; they must be proved. It must also be proved that the content of a vision and its formulation are beyond the grasp and abilities of the visionaries."

"The greatest mistake, however, is to expect visionaries (if there are more than 1), to relate their messages in exactly the same way. Subjectivity and differences in experiencing, receiving, transmitting, and explaining messages are not arguments against authenticity, but speak in its favor. To report a supernatural experience (such as a vision) 'objectively,' every individual must use his or her own expressions, metaphors, and descriptions (see Rahner's *Privatoffenbarung* 1963, p. 772). A good example of this is the 4 gospels in which the mystery of Christ is presented in different ways."

(Above quotations from the book, *The Apparitions of Our Lady of Medjugorje*, 1999, by Father Svetozar Kraljevic, published by the Information Centre "MIR" Medjugorje, pp. xv-xvii. Most of these points were taken from an article, "Vkazanja, Vidjenja, Objavc," investigation of the events in Medjugorje, appointed by the [then] bishop of Mostar, Msgr. Pavao Žanić.) [180]

Endnotes

Prologue

1. Biblegateway.com, New International Version (NIV), Old Testament, Isaiah 7:14.

2. Biblegateway.com, New American Standard Bible (NASB), New Testament, Gospel of Luke 1:32-35.

3. Biblegateway.com, NIV 1984, New Testament, Gospel of John, chapter 2.

4. Ibid, NIV 1984, Gospel of John, chapter 2.

5. Ibid, NIV 1984, Gospel of John, chapter 2.

6. Ibid, NIV 1984, Gospel of John, chapter 2.

7. Ibid, NIV, New Testament, Gospel of Matthew 7:21.

8. Ibid, NIV, Gospel of Matthew 7:23.

9. Ibid, NIV 1984, New Testament, Gospel of John 19:26-27.

10. Ibid, NIV 1984, New Testament, Gospel of John 19:26-27.

11. http://www.msnbc.msn.com/id/43727793/ns/world_news-world_environment/t/already-costliest-year-natural disasters

12. *The Network News* (N. Easton, MA: Medjugorje in America, June 2006), 1.

Introduction

13. www. medjugorje.hr. The figure reported as of the end of 2011 is 28,149,840 distributions of Holy Communion from 1985-2011 (beginning with 482,200 in 1985 and ending with 2,027,900 for 2011). To navigate the site (from the home page), click on "Medjugorje Phenomenon" at the top bar. On the next page, click "Statistics" from the left column. On the next page, choose "Distribution of Holy Communions" from the drop-down menu. Just below that, choose "Per Year" and "Total" from the next two drop-down menus, respectively.

14. Karl Rahner, SJ, *Visionen und Prophezeiungen* (1958), Freiburg im Breisgau: Herder & Co, GmbH; Third edition (1958), 24.

15. Ibid., 27

16. Ibid., 27

17. Biblegateway.com, NASB

18. *New American Bible (St. Joseph edition),revised edition* © 2010, 1991, 1986, 1970 Confraternity of Christian Doctrine, Washington, D.C.

Chapter 1

19. multiple sources:

Fr. Rene Laurentin, *Learning From Medjugorje*, (The Word Among Us Press, 1988).

Mary Craig, *Spark From Heaven*, (Ave Maria Press, 1988).

www. medjugorje.com, article: "Day One of the Apparitions, June 24, 1981, the Feast of St. John the Baptist."

www. medjugorjetoday.tv article: "Overview: The First Days, June 24, 1981"

Fr. Svetozar Kraljevic, *The Apparitions of Our Lady at Medjugorje*, 3rd edition, (Medjugorje: Information Center 'MIR,'

Medjugorje, 2010)., excerpts taken from interviews with Ivanka and Vicka in 1982 and 1983

20. multiple sources: Kraljevic, *The Apparitions of Our Lady of Medjugorje*

Laurentin, *Learning From Medjugorje*

Craig, *Spark From Heaven*

Stipe Cavar, *The First Months of the Apparitions in Medjugorje*, (Ziral Press, 2000).

www. medjugorje.com, article: "Day Two of the Apparitions," June 25, 1981

www. medjugorjetoday.tv, article: "Overview: The First Days, June 25, 1981"

21. NIV, New Testament, Gospel of John 20:29.

22. multiple sources: Kraljevic, *The Apparitions of Our Lady of Medjugorje*

Fr. Janko Bubalo, *A Thousand Encounters with the Blessed Virgin Mary in Medjugorje* (Chicago: Friends of Medjugorje Press, 1987)

Randall Sullivan, *The Miracle Detective* (Grove Press, 2004).

Craig, *Spark From Heaven*

www. medjugorje.com, article: "Day Three of the Apparitions," June 26, 1981

www. medjugorjetoday.tv, article: "Overview: The First Days, June 26, 1981"

23. Jan Connell, *Queen of the Cosmos* (Brewster, Massachusetts: Paraclete Press, 1990), 4.

24. Father Richard Foley, SJ, *The Drama of Medjugorje* (Veritas Publications, 1992), 12.

25. Jan Connell, *Queen of the Cosmos*, 4

26. www. medjugorje.hr—from the home page, click on "Medjugorje Phenomenon" from the top bar. On the next page, click on "Statistics" from the left column. On the next page, from the drop-down menu, choose "Distribution of Holy Communions." From the next two drop-down menus (same page), you must click on "Per Year" and "Total," respectively. The figure reported at the end of 2011 is 28,149,840 distributions of Holy Communion from 1985-2011 (beginning with 482,200 in 1985 and ending with 2,027,900 for 2011)

27. www. medjugorje.hr—from the home page, click on "Medjugorje Phenomenon" from the top bar. From the first drop-down menu on the "Statistics" page, choose "Concelebrating Priests." From the next drop-down menu, choose "Per Year." From the third drop-down menu, choose "Sva govorna podrucja" for the total.

Statistics showed 27,377 priests concelebrated in 2002; 27,498 in 2003; 28,166 in 2004; 29,673 in 2005; 32,094 in 2006; 34,265 in 2007; 30,238 in 2008; 33,302 in 2009; 38,227 in 2010; and 41,094 in 2011, totaling 321,934 for the ten-year period 2002-2011.

[28.] A Friend of Medjugorje, *Words From Heaven* (7th edition), (Sterrett, AL: St. James Publishing by Caritas of Birmingham, 1996), 160.

[29.] A Friend of Medjugorje, *American History You Never Learned* (Birmingham, AL: St. James Publishing, 2006), 5. Over 11,689 apparitions reported.

[30.] Sr. Emmanuel and Mr. Denis Nolan, *Medjugorje and the Church*, (Notre Dame, IN: United for the Triumph of the Immaculate Heart, 1995).

[31.] Dr. Ljudevit Rupčić, *The Truth about Medjugorje* (Ljubuski, Bosnia and Herzegovina: Ljudevit Rupčić, 1990), 111.

[32.] A Friend of Medjugorje, *Words from Heaven*, 248.

Chapter 2

[33.] *The Network News* (N. Easton, MA: Medjugorje in America, May 2006), 1.

[34.] St. Joseph edition of the New American Bible, Old Testament, Psalm 150:3-6.

[35.] Ibid, Psalm 98:4-6.

[36.] A Friend of Medjugorje, *Words From Heaven*, 244-45.

Chapter 3

37. www. spiritdaily.net/medjcures.htm,site visited 09/12/2012

38. Ibid.

39. www. medjugorjetoday.tv/3100/at-least-532-have-been-healed-in-medjugorje

40. www. catholicdaily.net/ourcatholicworld/2011/10/28/532-documented-healings-at-medjugorje

41. www. spiritdaily.net/medjcures.htm

42. Ibid

43. www. abcnews.go.com/GMA/living/story?id=247368&page=1, site visited 09/25/12

44. www. medjugorje.ws/en/apparitions/docs-medjugorje-miracles

45. www. medjugorje.com/medjugorje/signs-and-miracles/540-testimonies

46. www. medjugorje.com/medjugorje/signs-and-miracles/541-vickas-healing

47. Ibid.

48. Ibid.

49. A Friend of Medjugorje, *Words From Heaven*, 110.

50. Ibid, 102.

51. Ibid.

52. Ibid.109

53. Ibid.102

54. Ibid. 107

55. Ibid. 109

56. Ibid.

57. Ibid.

58. "Part I: The Apparitions," Wayne A. Weible, *Weible Columns: Miracle at Medjugorje*, Myrtle Beach, SC, 1986

    www. Medjugorje.org/wpart1.htm

Chapter 4

59. Father Richard Foley, SJ, *The Drama of Medjugorje*, 55.

60. Ibid.

61. Ibid, 56.

62. Sr. Emmanuel and Mr. Denis Nolan, *Medjugorje and the Church*, 5-6.

63. www.medjugorje.com/medjugorje/beginning-days-of-the-apparitions.html, "Day Four of the Apparitions: June 27, 1981."

64. Kraljevic, *The Apparitions of Our Lady at Medjugorje*.

65. Ibid.

66. www.medjugorje.com/medjugorje/beginning-days-of-the-apparitions.html, "Day Four of the Apparitions: June 27, 1981."

67. Ibid

68. combined sources: Kraljevic, *The Apparitions of Our Lady at Medjugorje* www. medjugorjetoday.tv/background-7/the-first-days/june-27ᵗʰ/

69. combined sources: Kraljevic, *The Apparitions of Our Lady at Medjugorje* www. medjugorjetoday.tv/background-7/the-first-days/june-27ᵗʰ/

70. www. biblegateway.com, NASB, Matthew 12:38-40

71. Ibid.

72. www.medjugorje.hr---from the home page click tab at top "Medjugorje Phenomenon." On the next page, click tab (on left side of page) "Statistics." On Statistics page, click on "Distribution of Holy Communions" from the drop-down menu. From the next two drop-down menus, click on "Per Year" and "Total," respectively. The following stats are reported for 2002-2011:1,138,000 hosts (2002); 1,179,000 (2003); 1,224,000 (2004); 1,299,100 (2005); 1,451,100 (2006); 1,608,100 (2007); 1,357,100 (2008); 1,378,600 (2009); 1,571,800 (2010); 2,027,900 (2011).

73. www.medjugorje.hr, click tab (top of page) "Medjugorje Phenomenon." On the next page click tab (on left side of page) "Statistics." On Statistics page, from the first drop-down menu, click on "Concelebrating Priests." For the next two drop-down menus, you must click on "Per Year" and "Sva govorna podrucja" (annual figure): 27,377 (2002); 27,498 (2003); 28,188 (2004); 29,673 (2005); 32,094 (2006); 34,265 (2007); 30,238 (2008); 33,302 (2009); 38,227 (2010); and 41,094 (2011).

74. A Friend of Medjugorje, *Words From Heaven*, 282.

Chapter 5

75. A Friend of Medjugorje, *Words From Heaven*, 88.

76. Ibid, 89

77. Ibid, 89

78. Ibid, 89

79. Ibid, 90

80. Ibid, 90

81. Ibid, 91

82. Ibid, 91

83. Ibid, 92

84. From www.medjugorje.hr, the official website for Medjugorje: Place of Prayer and Reconciliation. Click on "Medjugorje Phenomenon" on the bar at the top of home page. When this page comes up, click on "Our Lady's Messages" from the menu on the left side of the screen. Then, the caption "Introduction to the Messages" will appear immediately below that. Click on that and you will find a summary account of early apparitions and the five messages by Dr. Fr. Ljudevit Rupčić. Scroll about halfway down the article down to "Messages." Here you will find the section written about peace, faith, conversion, prayer, and fasting

85. Ibid.

86. A Friend of Medjugorje, *Words From Heaven*, 244.

87. Ibid.

Chapter 6

88. A Friend of Medjugorje, *Words From Heaven*, 243.

89. Ibid, 49.

90. Ibid.

91. Ibid.

92. Father Richard Foley, SJ, *The Drama of* Medjugorje, 90.

93. A Friend of Medjugorje, *Words From Heaven*, 138-139.

94. Ibid, 50-51.

95. Ibid, 55-57.

96. Ibid, 53-54.

97. Ibid, 51.

98. Ibid, 51-52.

99. Ibid, 117.

100. Ibid, 55.

101. Ibid, 54.

102. Ibid, vii.

103. Father Richard Foley, SJ, *The Drama of Medjugorje*, 90.

Chapter 7

104. www.blessedmotherguideus.wordpress.com/2010/10/20/the-popes-haunting-echo-of-medjugorje/

105. St. Joseph edition of the New American Bible, Revised New Testament of the New American Bible.

106. A Friend of Medjugorje, *Words From Heaven*, 282.

Chapter 8

107. A Friend of Medjugorje, *Words From Heaven*, 341

108. "Part I: The Apparitions," *Weible Columns: Miracle at Medjugorje*

109. A Friend of Medjugorje, *Words From Heaven*, 171.

110. "Part I: "The Apparitions," *Weible Columns: Miracle at Medjugorje*

111. "Part VI: "Update on Medjugorje," *Weible Columns: Miracle at Medjugorje*

112. St. Joseph edition of the New American Bible, Revised New Testament of the New American Bible, Matthew 24:7-8.

113. Ibid, Matthew 24:30.

114. Ibid, Matthew 24:37-42.

115. Jan Connell. *Queen of the Cosmos*, 134.

[116.] St. Joseph edition of the New American Bible, Revised New Testament of the New American Bible, Matthew 25:41.

[117.] Ibid, Revelation 8:4, 6-7.

[118.] Ibid, Revelation 21:1.

[119.] A Friend of Medjugorje, *Words From Heaven*, 171.

Chapter 9

[120.] St. Joseph edition of the New American Bible, Old Testament, Exodus 20:1-17.

[121.] Ibid, Exodus 20:15.

[122.] St. Joseph edition of the New American Bible, Old Testament, Exodus 20:12.

[123.] Ibid, Revised New Testament of the New American Bible, 1 John 1:8.

[124.] Ibid, Romans 3:23.

[125.] Ibid, Romans 10:9.

[126] http://www.medjugorjelive.org/index.php/component/content/article/1178-message-to-mirjana-may-2-2011, website accessed, August 14, 2012

Chapter 10

[127.] St. Joseph edition of the New American Bible, Revised New Testament of the New American Bible, John 14:15.

128. St. Joseph edition of the New American Bible, Old Testament.

129. Ibid, Revised New Testament of the New American Bible, Matthew 5:27-28.

130. Ibid, Matthew 5:1-7:29.

131. St. Joseph edition of the New American Bible, Old Testament, Exodus 20:13.

132. Ibid, Revised New Testament of the New American Bible, Matthew 5:22.

133. Ibid, Ephesians 4:26-27

134. www.spiritdaily.com/mirjanamessageapril07.htm

Chapter 11

135. "French-Italian Scientific Theological Commission on the extraordinary events that are taking place in Medjugorje," via www. medjugorje.hr. To view scientific studies, click on "Medjugorje Phenomenon" on the top bar. On the page that comes up, click on "MEDJUGORJE IN THE CHURCH" in the left column. On that page, look down the items to the last one which says SCIENTIFIC RESEARCHES. Click on "Commissions and Teams." This commission's report will be the first study shown on the page.

136. Ibid

137. Father Rene Laurentin, *Is the Virgin Mary Appearing at Medjugorje?* (Washington DC: The Word Among Us Press, 1984), 135.

138. Ibid.

139. Ibid, 135-136.

140. Sr. Emmanuel and Mr. Denis Nolan, *Medjugorje and the Church*, 19.

141. Ibid, 4

www.medjugorje.hr.
(from the website www.medjugorje.hr: "Monsignor Maurillo Kreiger, former bishop of Florianopolis (Brazil) visited Medjugorje four times. He writes, "I told the Pope I am going to Medjugorje for the fourth time." He (the pope) concentrated his thoughts and said, "Medjugorje Medjugorje, it's the spiritual heart of the world." The book *Medjugorje and the Church* report the 1990 incident similarly: (from Bishop Murilo Krieger, Brazil, for publication in the National Catholic Register USA) the bishop stated, "I spoke with the Holy Father on the 24th of February 1990. I told him I had been to Medjugorje 3 times and that I was going to return the following week. He said simply: 'Medjugorje is a great center of spirituality.'"

142. Sr. Emmanuel and Mr. Denis Nolan, *Medjugorje and the Church*

www.medjugorje.hr
(from www.medjugorje.hr. It is written that Msgr. Kim, president of the Korean Bishops' Conference, published an article November 11, 1990, in the Korean national weekly newspaper *Catholic News*. In the article, he wrote the following: "Prior to the conclusion of the last Bishops' Synode in Rome, the Korean bishops were invited to a lunch with the Holy Father. On this occasion, Msgr. Kim addressed the Holy Father directly and said, 'Father, thanks to you, Poland was able to liberate itself from Communism.' To this, the Holy Father responded, 'No, this is not my merit. This is the work of the Blessed Virgin Mary, as she had predicted in Fatima and in Medjugorje.' *Medjugorje and the Church* reported, "Archbishop Angelo Kim, President of the Korean Episcopal Conference, reported in the Korean Catholic weekly, 11th of November, 1990, the following dialogue with John Paul II: 'Thanks to you, Poland has now been

freed from Communism.' The Pope replied, 'No, not me, but by the works of the Blessed Virgin according to her affirmations at Fatima and Medjugorje.'"

143. Sr. Emmanuel and Mr. Denis Nolan, *Medjugorje and the Church*

www.medjugorje.hr
(from www. medjugorje.hr: "The Archbishop of Paraguay, Msgr. Felipe Santiago Bentez, in November of 1994 asked of the Holy Father if he was right to give approval to the faithful gathering in the spirit of Medjugorje, especially with the priests of Medjugorje. The Holy Father answered: 'Approve all that is related to Medjugorje.'" This rather all-encompassing approval is reported very similarly in *Medjugorje and the Church*: "In autumn, 1994, several Centers for Peace were preparing an apostolic tour for Father Slavko Barbaric (a Franciscan priest stationed in Medjugorje). This was to take place in South America for Jan-Feb 1995. The Archbishop of Ascuncion, Paraguay, Msgr. Felipe Santiago Benitez, hesitated. He wasn't sure that he should allow gatherings about Medjugorje in the churches. He therefore requested letters of recommendation about Father Slavko from the Provincial of the Franciscans and the Bishop of Mostar. As he was in Rome in November 1994, he asked the Pope whether or not it was appropriate to give permission for these meetings in the spirit of Medjugorje to take place—particularly with a priest from Medjugorje. The Holy Father answered: 'Authorize everything that concerns Medjugorje!' Archbishop Benitez then considered it unnecessary to receive any other recommendations. He called the Center for Peace and gave them permission, for the Pope himself had said to do so!"

144. Sr. Emmanuel and Mr. Denis Nolan, *Medjugorje and the Church*, 1.

145. Ibid, 1-2.

146. www.medjugorje.org/wordpress/archives/38, "Holy See Established International Commission for Medjugorje."

147. www.medjugorje.hr. Information Centre "MIR" Medjugorje—from home page, click on link "Medjugorje Phenomenon" from the top bar. On next page, click on "Medjugorje in the Church" from the menu on the left. On the next page, click on the caption which begins with "Zadar Declaration, Commentary of the Declaration ..."

148. Sr. Emmanuel and Mr. Denis Nolan, *Medjugorje and the Church*, 4

149. www. medjugorje.hr. On the home page, click on "Medjugorje Phenomenon" from the top bar. On next page, click on "Our Lady's Messages" from menu in column on left. On the next page, click on "1991" from the table on the right side of the page. Then, immediately beneath that, click on "7" and "8" for months of July and August, respectively, to find messages for July 25, 1991 and August 25, 1991

150. Sr. Emmanuel and Mr. Denis Nolan, *Medjugorje and the Church*, 4

151. Ibid, 6

152. Dr. Ljudevit Rupčić, *The Truth about Medjugorje* (Ljubuski, Bosnia and Herzegovina: Ljudevit Rupčić, 1990), 72.

153. Ibid.

154. Ibid, 73.

155. Ibid, 111

156. Ibid, 107-108

157. Ibid. 111

158. Rev. David du Plessis, *Simple and Profound* (Brewster, Massachusetts: Paraclete Press, 1985), 198

159. St. Joseph edition of the New American Bible, Revised New Testament of the New American Bible, John 20:25.

160. Ibid, John 20:27-29

161. www. medjugorje.hr. On the home page, click on "Medjugorje Phenomenon" from the top bar. On next page, click on "Our Lady's Messages" from menu in column on left. On the next page, click on "2007" from the table on the right side of the page. Then, immediately beneath that, click on "8" to retrieve the message of August 25, 2007.

Chapter 12

162. A Friend of Medjugorje, *Words From Heaven, 160.*

163. www.medjugorje.org/comm/sb0807.htm.

164. St. Joseph edition of the New American Bible, Revised New Testament of the New American Bible, Matthew 11:28.

165. A Friend of Medjugorje, *Words From Heaven*, 243

166. Ibid, 243-249.

167. St. Joseph edition of the New American Bible, Revised New Testament of the New American Bible, Matthew 7:9.

168. A Friend of Medjugorje, *Words From Heaven*, 89

169. St. Joseph edition of the New American Bible, Revised New Testament of the New American Bible, Matthew 6:9-15.

170. A Friend of Medjugorje, *Words From Heaven*, 245.

171. St. Joseph edition of the New American Bible, Revised New Testament of the New American Bible.

172. www.medjugorje.hr. On the home page, click on "Medjugorje Phenomenon" from the top bar. On next page, click on "Our Lady's Messages" from menu in column on left. On the next page, click on "2008" from the table on the right side of the page. Then, immediately beneath that, click on "9" to retrieve the message of September 25, 2008.

Appendix 1

173. Father Richard Foley, SJ, *The Drama of Medjugorje*, 133.

174. Ibid, 134

175. Jan Connell. *Queen of the Cosmos: Interviews with the Visionaries of Medjugorje*, 63-66.

176. Ibid, 93-94.

Appendix 2

177. www. medjugorje.hr—from the home page, click on "Medjugorje Phenomenon" from the bar at the top. On the next page, click on "Medjugorje in the Church" from the column on the left. At the bottom of list on next page, look under "Scientific Researches." Click on "Commissions and Teams"

Appendix 3

178. www.medjugorje.hr. Information Centre "MIR" Medjugorje—from home page, click on link "Medjugorje Phenomenon" from the top

bar. On next page, click on "Medjugorje in the Church" from the bar on the left. On the next page, click on the caption which begins with "Zadar Declaration, Commentary of the Declaration …"

Appendix 4

179. "Step-by-Step Instructions for Praying the Rosary," "Various Rosary Prayers …," "The Fifteen Promises …," and "Why the Daily Rosary" adapted and modified from www.catholic.org (Catholic Online).

Appendix 5

180. Kraljevic, *The Apparitions of Our Lady of Medjugorje*, (Medjugorje: Information Centre "MIR," 1999), xv-xvii.